HOW TO
CLIMB A MOUNTAIN

Simon Pearce

First published in Great Britain 2024 by Pesda Press

Tan y Coed Canol

Ceunant

Caernarfon

Gwynedd

LL55 4RN

© Copyright 2024 Simon Pearce

ISBN: 978-1-906095-93-2

Printed and bound in Poland, hussarbooks.pl

FSC

MIX

Paper from
responsible sources

FSC® C167221

"You are not in the mountains. The mountains are in you."

- John Muir

Acknowledgements

I'm hugely thankful to so many people who've helped me in my mountaineering career and in writing this book. It would be impossible to list them all. What I love most about being in the mountains is that everyone you meet is friendly and helpful, so when coming to write this book it was easy to call on the support of friends and colleagues.

Thank you to the following who have provided help, advice, photographs and more in the compiling of this book: Lawrie Brand, Lyle Brotherton, Alex Croall, Tony Ellis, Franco Ferrero, Rich Griffiths, Andy Hewlett, Bill Hilton, Tammy Holmes, Keith Hulse, Carla Imbrenda, Belinda Kirk, Harriet MacMillan, Serena and Evan Pearce, Mike Raine, Nick Read, Richard Rees, Tom Swinhoe, Hywel Watkin, Kev Williams and Katherine Wills.

I would also like to thank all the clients of MountainXperience who have put up with me taking umpteen photos of them over the years.

All images are by the author except where acknowledged in the caption.

About the Author

Simon's love of the outdoors began in Cubs where he always enjoyed exploring – but later, as a Venture Scout, he visited the Peak District and didn't really enjoy getting drenched while wild camping! Some twenty years later he rediscovered his love of the outdoors, and in particular map reading. Short, local hill walks quickly turned into longer and more adventurous days out as he found higher and more exciting things to climb. A few outdoor courses later and Simon went on to gain numerous leadership and coaching qualifications in mountaineering and paddlesports.

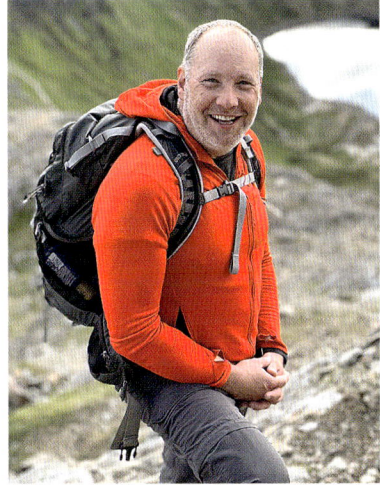

In recent years, Simon has worked for a large outdoor charity with responsibility for the training and wellbeing of its volunteers, and as Chief Operating Officer of an adventure travel company, developing new and exciting holidays for its clients.

Today, Simon works full time in the outdoors running his own mountaineering business, based in North Wales but operating around the UK. MountainXperience guides hundreds of people safely to the summit of Yr Wyddfa (Snowdon) each year and teaches others how to stay safe in the hills and mountains on various outdoor training courses.

His personal mountaineering career has seen him climb mountains on four continents, but he mostly loves exploring what we have here in the UK. Even after years spent in the outdoors, there are still British adventures he's keen to tackle.

Simon particularly enjoys working with those new to the outdoors and is passionate about passing on outdoor skills to others. He's a provider and course director for Mountain Training and delivers their Hill and Mountain Skills courses in Eryri (Snowdonia) and the Peak District. He also loves teaching map reading and compass skills as a provider and course tutor for the National Navigation Award Scheme.

Find out more about how you can join the author and his team on the mountain or on an upcoming outdoor course at *www.mountainxperience.uk*.

Contents

Contents

Route Maps and Guides

Appendices

A group stood at the summit of Yr Wyddfa (Snowdon) admiring the views.

Introduction

For most of you reading these words, this represents the beginning of your mountain climbing journey. I hope you're as excited as I was when I first started dreaming of mountains. What I most love about climbing mountains is that it's an adventure every time. It doesn't matter if you're seven years old and running up your local hill, or 77 years old climbing Kilimanjaro, it's an adventure, and it's that adventure that makes it exciting.

I find myself climbing Yr Wyddfa (Snowdon) around 70 times a year for work and it's still an adventure every time. I meet new people, I still see new sights, and I always experience something different. Most importantly, I come off the mountain each time with a smile on my face. That's an adventure in my books.

This book is all about **you** starting **your** adventure. You might be a parent looking to take the family on a weekend in the hills, or perhaps you've been roped into a charity challenge at work to climb the National Three Peaks, or maybe you've signed up to summit Toubkal in Africa or hike to Everest Base Camp. I'm here to help you plan for your adventure. I'll tell you what you need to know before you start, everything you'll want to have with you, how to plan your trip and, most importantly, how to stay safe.

Adventure Revolution

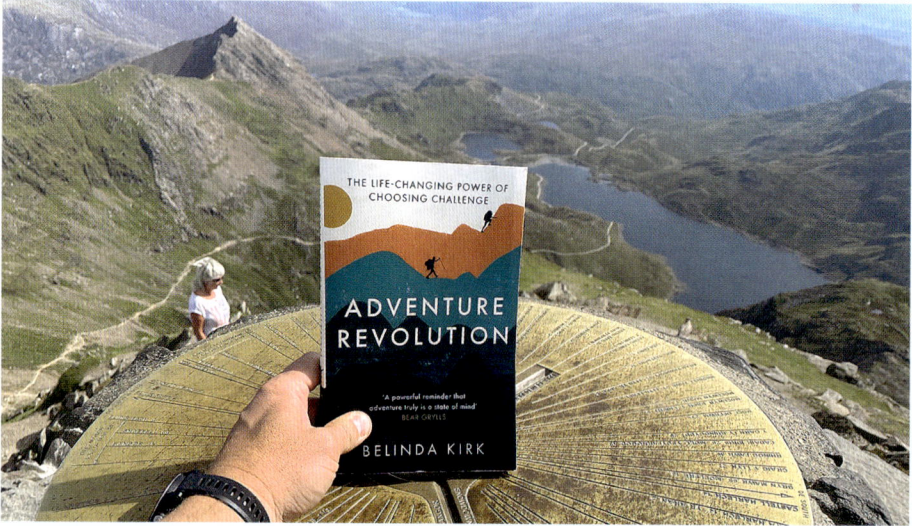

Lookng down from the summit of Yr Wyddfa (Snowdon) towards Llyn Llydaw – Crib Goch on top left.

If you'd like to read more about how adventure changes lives, I highly recommend a book by my former boss Belinda Kirk: Adventure Revolution: The life-changing power of choosing challenge.

Belinda is an explorer and leading campaigner promoting the benefits of adventure on wellbeing. Over the past twenty-five years, she has led dozens of international expeditions and remote filming trips. Belinda has walked through Nicaragua, sailed across the Atlantic, searched for camels in China's Desert of Death, discovered ancient rock paintings in Lesotho and, with the other members of the crew, gained a Guinness World Record for rowing unsupported around Britain.

With much of Belinda's professional life revolving around adventure she's seen it change people first hand, turning the timid into the confident, the addicted into the recovering, and the lost into the intentionally wandering. This book reveals the astonishing health and psychological benefits of living more adventurously.

If you're new to mountain walking you can read this book from start to finish, but then I suggest keeping it close to hand as a useful reference guide for you to dip in and out of. The chapters are designed for you to quickly and easily find an answer to any mountain climbing query.

What I've written here is really aimed at those new to the outdoors. If you're ready to plan your first mountain climbing adventure, read on.

The UK's most popular mountain, Yr Wyddfa (Snowdon) in North Wales. Could this be your mountain climbing target?

1 Getting Started

Why do we climb mountains? This is something my non-mountain friends challenge me over frequently, and something I'm not always able to persuade them about. But almost without fail, every time I'm stood on a mountain summit, I'm overcome by a huge sense of achievement. Even if it's a mountain I've climbed many times before, or if the weather is rubbish and I'm soaked, or if we got lost on the way up and it took an hour longer than planned; I've still achieved something that most others haven't.

You too can have that sense of achievement, and it's something you can have regularly. What I most envy about you, the reader, is that you're at the start of your mountain climbing career and have the opportunity to achieve so much still ahead of you. Taking your toddlers out to climb a local hill, organising a family trip to something bigger, or planning your own major international mountain ascent – the achievements are out there and waiting for you.

You don't need to be an expert mountain navigator (although knowing the basics will help – see Chapter 10), you don't need to be super fit (read more in Chapter 3) and you don't need all the latest expensive gear (see what you do need in Chapters 7 and 8). Climbing a mountain might not be as hard as you think, so begin the path to your next mountain achievement today.

Crib Goch ridge – perhaps best left until you have gained more experience.

British Mountaineering Council Participation Statement

Tho Britioh Mountainccring Council (DMC) is the representative body that exists to protect the freedoms and promote the interests of climbers, hill walkers and mountaineers. Its 'Participation Statement' sums up pretty well the risks involved in climbing mountains. Of course, we do everything we can to help mitigate these risks (reading this book being the first thing!) but it's important to know that these risks exist.

The BMC Participation Statement states that: The BMC recognises that climbing and mountaineering are activities with a danger of personal injury or death. Participants in these activities should be aware of and accept these risks and be responsible for their own actions.

Mountain climbers standing on top of Ben A'an in the Scottish Highlands.   Photo: Andreaobzerova, Dreamstime.com

2 What is a Mountain?

Surprisingly, there isn't actually a universally accepted definition of what a mountain is. If, like me, you grew up in rural Lincolnshire, you could be amazed when you come across any size hill; whereas someone brought up in the Swiss Alps might come to the UK and scoff at our highest point being just 1,345m (4,413ft) high.

In the UK and Ireland, the official Government definition of a mountain is a summit of 610m (2,000ft), or higher. There are other requirements relating to prominence and isolation but I wouldn't worry about them.

Using this definition, there are over 2,700 mountains in the British Isles with 80% being in Scotland, 8% in Ireland, 7% in England and 5% in Wales. While you're going to have to travel up to the Scottish Highlands to climb the really big ones, the rest are scattered right across the UK and you're sure to have something nearby.

You'll hear people talking about Munros, Corbetts and Wainwrights. These are just a few of the many different classifications of our hills and mountains in the UK. Unless you plan on taking on one of the popular challenges such as climbing all 214 Lake District Wainwrights, or summiting the 282 Scottish Munros, I wouldn't worry too much about all the technical terms. However, a particularly good collection is the 'Trail 100' where the experts at the UK hillwalking publication Trail Magazine have compiled the 'definitive collection of the 100 UK peaks all hillwalkers must climb at least once in their life'. Search for it online, find your nearest peak and start planning your adventure.

Trail 100 Challenge

Hand-picked by the experts at Trail Magazine, the Trail 100 will take you from the mighty summits of Scotland to the limestone peaks of the Yorkshire Dales and the gritstone edges of the Peak District. You'll cross razor-sharp Welsh ridges, lose yourself in Lakeland valleys, explore the weird tors of Dartmoor, discover the dazzling green beauty of the Brecon Beacons, and reach the highest point in Ireland's Mourne Mountains. You can find the full Trail 100 list in the appendix.

If you're really interested in learning more about each individual hill and mountain, look for The Database of British and Irish Hills online, where a small group of committed statisticians maintain an accurate database – a 'user friendly' version of which can be accessed at www.hill-bagging.co.uk.

Don't get too hung up on whether something is a hill or a mountain, or neither. If you've had a good time, climbed something, got your boots dirty and worn yourself out then, as far as I'm concerned, that's a good mountain day.

What is 'mountain climbing'?

This is a matter of regular online debate. What exactly is the difference between hiking, trekking, hillwalking, mountain climbing and mountaineering? There isn't a hard and fast rule about which word describes a particular activity, and the terms are used interchangeably in everyday language. If you want my opinion (and you obviously do otherwise you wouldn't have bought my book), I'd suggest the increase in activity level, and perhaps difficulty, goes in the order they're written above.

A 'walk' is what you do to get to the bus stop. It's how you get from A to B and is incidental to what you're trying to do.

A 'hike' is a walk with the purpose of activity or exercise. It would usually be in the countryside but can also be around town. What differentiates it from simply walking is that the hiking is the main activity. You might also start to introduce activity specific gear such as a rucksack or proper hiking boots – stuff you wouldn't normally have for a walk.

Scrambling the awesome Crib Goch ridge up to Yr Wyddfa (Snowdon). I defy anyone to tell me this isn't 'climbing'!

A 'trek' is a considerable 'hike' – possibly even overnight (although we might also call this backpacking). You'll have equipment with you to last more than just a few hours, and you'll definitely look the part with dedicated outdoor clothing and a rucksack on your back. Trekking lets you explore further by not necessarily having to be back where you started at the end of the day.

'Hillwalking' and 'mountain climbing' for me are the two most 'blurred' terms and are frequently used to describe the activity of going up a mountain on foot. 'Hillwalking' could lend itself more to gentler terrain and perhaps familiar paths, and one could argue that 'mountain climbing' is a more serious experience, but in everyday language I'd suggest there's little between them. All that aside, the official Mountain Training handbook for professional Mountain Leaders is called Hill Walking, which further adds to the debate!

Next up would be 'scrambling', which is often an ambiguous term for activities that sit between hillwalking and mountaineering / rock climbing. Here, you'll be using your hands as well as your feet, and with the added levels of excitement come added risks. Scrambles, even simple ones, by their very nature are often high, narrow and exposed. Some of the best examples of 'easy' UK scrambles are the Crib Goch arête on Yr Wyddfa (Snowdon) in North Wales, Striding Edge on Helvellyn in the Lake District and the

Sunrise over the Mourne Mountains in Northern Ireland.   *Photo: Sara Winter, Dreamstime.com*

Carn Mor Dearg arête on Ben Nevis in the Scottish Highlands. These are all classed as Grade I scrambles, meaning that no special equipment is necessarily required. However, if you're reading this book then they're probably still a little way off for you, without the assistance of a qualified mountain guide. Certainly, once you move in to Grade II and III scrambles, the crossover in to rock climbing becomes a lot more blurred.

What is definitely a step up for most people would be 'mountaineering'. At this level we're starting to introduce special equipment such as ropes and harnesses, and we're well in to 'rock climbing' territory. This is not something I'm going to go into in this book, as it's definitely not for those new to the outdoors.

So, do we actually 'climb' a mountain?

In the English language today, it's widely accepted that to 'climb a mountain' is to make an ascent in whatever way you feel. So, whether you used ropes and harnesses to scale a rock face or just your feet on a long, uphill walk then, great job – you've climbed a mountain!

Do as much as you can to be prepared for your mountain climbing experience.   Photo: Anna Dudko, Dreamstime.com

3 Are You Fit Enough?

You might be put off the idea of climbing a mountain because you don't think your fitness is up to scratch. It is true that reaching the summit of many mountains around the world is a real physical and mental challenge, and an individual's fitness level is subjective – but taking the routes in the back of this book as an example, none of these are out of the realm of most of you reading this now. Preparation is key, and certainly, the more ready you are for your mountain day, the easier it's going to be, and therefore the more likely you are to enjoy it.

I regularly work with people with little or no mountain walking experience, and lead them successfully to a summit, and back down again. Some are active gym-goers, many are keen walkers and even runners but, unless you're regularly walking up something, you're likely to find a big mountain somewhat of an assault on your lower body.

Don't run before you can walk (metaphorically)

If you've done little or no serious distance walking and find yourself out of breath running up the stairs, you're probably going to struggle getting to the top of a mountain; putting in some good prep work is essential. You don't have to be an athlete, you don't need to be able to run a marathon, but you do need to be able to walk uphill for several hours and then back down again. I often meet people struggling their way up Wales' highest mountain, and when we stop and chat they tell me that not only is this their first ever mountain climb, but often it's the most physical exercise they've ever done in their life.

Don't assume just because Barry from marketing 'smashed Snowdon' last year, that it's necessarily going to be the same experience for you. We're all different. We all have different bodies and differing fitness levels. Put in the time and effort before your big mountain day and you're guaranteed a more positive experience.

Take the family out locally to get everyone used to walking – Lud's Church, Peak District.

Practise walking

It might sound daft, but the best thing you can do to prepare yourself for climbing a mountain is to get out and practise walking. You may not be able to venture uphill close to where you live but that doesn't stop you getting out and about on the flat. If you're just starting out, try going for a simple walk around your neighbourhood and aim to be active for as long as you feel able. You'll want to be comfortable walking for at least an hour and eventually for several hours; although I'd argue that if you get back from a 60-minute walk and you're still feeling good, then you're likely to be OK. Remember that on a mountain day you're going to be out all day. For example, you'll need six to eight hours to reach the summit of Yr Wyddfa (Snowdon) and get back down again.

As you progress on your local walks, start seeking out hills and inclines to begin to appreciate the difference between walking on the flat and walking uphill.

The more you can get your body used to walking good distances in advance of your first big mountain day, the better the day is likely to go.

Test your gear

As you progress and your fitness improves, you definitely want to try out your gear. If you've invested in new walking boots, you'll find yourself getting more tired wearing them than a normal pair of trainers as they are likely to weigh more; start wearing them on local walks to add a bit of realism. Add your rucksack too, and build up what you carry in it so it's not such a shock when you start on your first real mountain.

Make sure your waterproofs fit well over your walking clothes and that you can walk comfortably in them. Trying them on in the shop is fine but they need to feel good while you're moving, and for more than just a few minutes. If you use walking poles, try them out so you know how to extend and adjust them. Be sure your socks fit correctly and that they're warm enough / not too warm. All of these things become second nature after a while, but when you're starting out, you'll need to be a bit more aware.

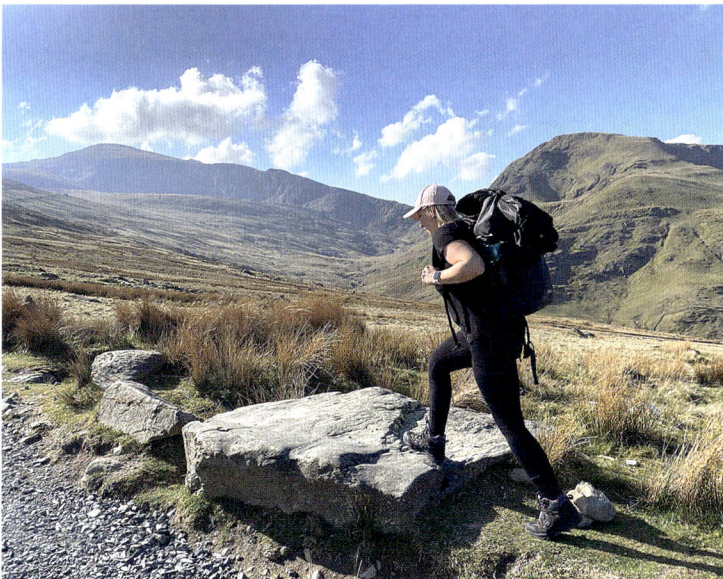

A well-equipped walker testing her new gear before a big mountain adventure.

Do some 'cardio'

As you start moving your 'practise walking' from the flat to uphill, you'll start to appreciate how much more energy is needed and how much harder your body is working. As with most physical activities, the more often you do something, the more your body will get used to it. There's no substitute for getting out and practising. However, if you're able to get to the gym, or if you can workout at home then regular cardiovascular exercise will do wonders for your mountain walking. Get your body moving, get your heart rate up, and get into a pattern of exercise. Since the pandemic I've become a big fan of home workouts which you can find through smartphone apps or even your smart TV. They're easy to do, relatively cheap and you don't even need to leave the house.

If you're planning to take on a major mountain then cardiovascular training is essential, as expeditions such as Kilimanjaro or Everest Base Camp will require consistent physical effort, day after day.

Move your body

I'm going to suggest two things that you're not going to like. Squats and lunges are brilliant ways of getting your lower body ready for climbing a mountain, or more particularly for dealing with coming back down again. You don't need to be knocking out 100 in one go, but doing a few daily exercises in the run-up to your big mountain day will make a huge difference. Many complain that they find descending more strenuous on their lower limbs than heading up the mountain, so anything you can do to prepare for this will help.

If you're looking for some easy workout ideas or just need a bit of motivation, check out daily challenges from websites such as darebee.com.

Take regular breaks

You should enjoy your mountain day at your pace. It's absolutely fine (and encouraged) to take breaks throughout your climb. Unless you're taking part in a mountain marathon, you're climbing a mountain for enjoyment, and sometimes we forget that, particularly if you're walking with a group.

Mountain summits aren't usually the best place to stop for a picnic lunch due to the weather, exposure, etc. Regular, shorter stops along the way ensure you stay fuelled and hydrated, and also give you an opportunity to recover.

However, as so often, there is a fine line here. If you find yourself sat in the Hafod Eryri visitor centre on top of Yr Wyddfa (Snowdon) relaxing with coffee and cake, do remember your day is only half done and you still have to get down the mountain. The longer you sit still, the more your body is going to seize up, so enjoy a shorter break and keep your momentum.

Pace yourself

It's important to find your mountain pace. This can be tricky when walking as part of a group but it's key to enjoying your mountain day.

If you find yourself struggling to hold a conversation because you're out of breath, then you're moving too fast. In this case, rather than stopping frequently to catch your breath, try walking a little slower. You should be able to chat with relative ease while you're on the go

Remember to take regular breaks and enjoy the views – Halfway House, Eryri (Snowdon).

Getting out with a local walking club is a great way to boost your fitness.

Join a walking club

There are groups of people all over the country who meet every week and go out walking together. These range from small gatherings planned on social media platforms such as Meetup or via local Facebook groups, to entire organisations that are dedicated to getting people outside. Many are free or they might have a monthly or annual membership fee. What they all offer is a great way to get / stay fit, enjoy the outdoors and make new friends.

Something to bear in mind, is that many smaller get-togethers organised online are typically peer-led events and there's unlikely to be any particular person in charge. This is somewhat of a grey area amongst the outdoor community where we would normally ensure that there's a qualified leader with up to date first aid training, public liability insurance, etc. If you're at all concerned, look for a larger, more organised walking group.

High up in the Peak District National Park in Derbyshire.   *Photo: Jasminelove, Dreamstime.com*

4 Where to Go

The UK is fortunate to have 15 national parks covering nearly 9,000 square miles of the country. They range from the New Forest on the South Coast, the Broads in East Anglia and Pembrokeshire in West Wales, up to the Cairngorms in the Northern Highlands of Scotland – so you're never going to be too far from one. Between them they welcome over 100 million visitors each year, and they're completely free of charge.

For people looking to climb a mountain, some will be more exciting than others (I've explored the Norfolk Broads as a child and loved it, but it's not quite the Himalayas). Most will have something for you to walk up, and as you build up your challenges, you'll be able to venture to new places.

What all national parks have in common is that they've been created for us all to explore and enjoy.

But where can you find your nearest mountain? Well, this can be a bit tricky and obviously depends on whereabouts in the UK you're based. The South of England is rather barren when it comes to mountains. You'll struggle to find anything much above 600m and you'll have to travel to Dartmoor in the South West to find that. If you're in the South East you'll not really be able to venture higher than a few hundred metres.

Britain's national parks

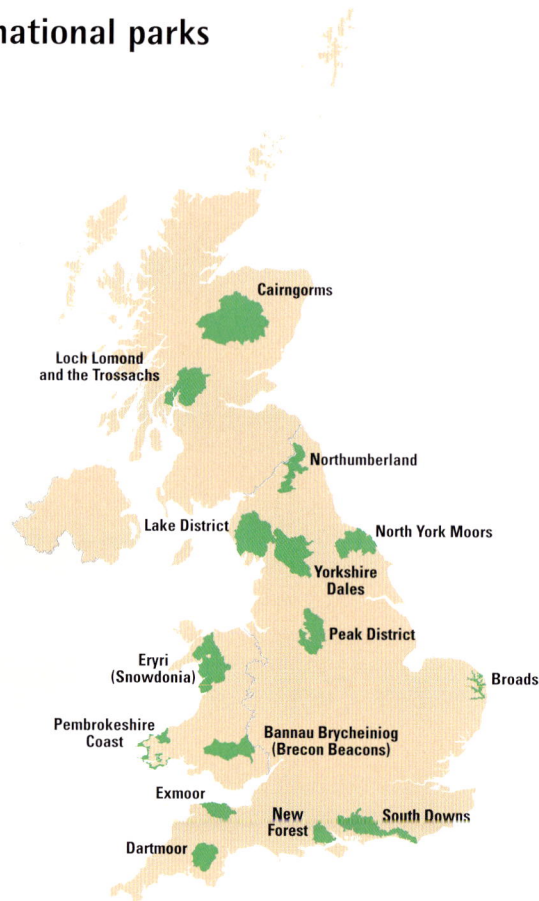

Cairngorms

Loch Lomond and the Trossachs

Northumberland

Lake District

North York Moors

Yorkshire Dales

Peak District

Eryri (Snowdonia)

Broads

Pembrokeshire Coast

Bannau Brycheiniog (Brecon Beacons)

Exmoor

New Forest

South Downs

Dartmoor

Map by Bute Cartographics. Contains OS data © Crown copyright and database rights 2023.

This is not to say these places aren't worth visiting; they will make excellent 'training' hills, but for the really big ones you're going to have to travel north. For anything above 1,000m you're going to have to go a long way north.

In England you should head for the Pennines and the Lake District. Wales has the Black Mountains and Bannau Brycheiniog (Brecon Beacons) in the south, the Cambrian Mountains and Berwyns in mid-Wales and the Clwydian Range and Eryri (Snowdonia) in the north. In Northern Ireland you have the Mourne Mountains, the Sperrins and the Antrim Hills.

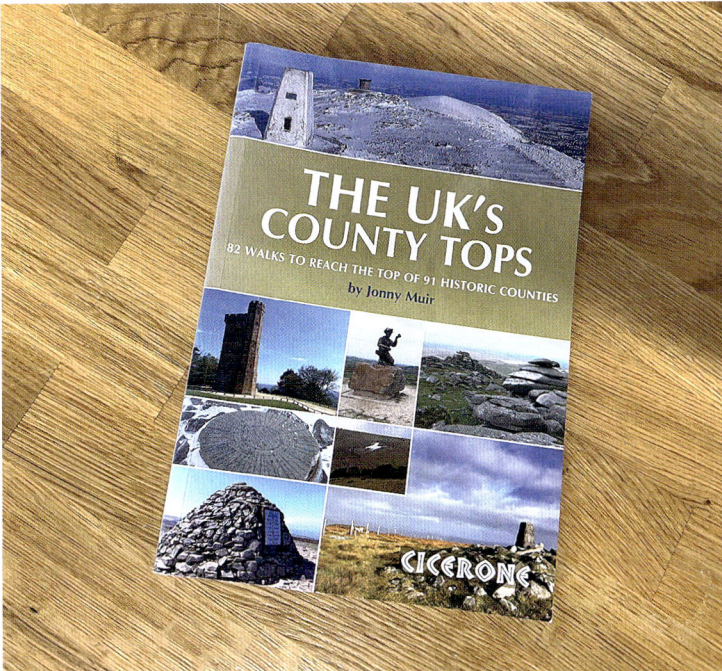

Books like this are great for finding things to climb near you.

But it's in Scotland where you'll find the biggest mountains the UK has to offer; the Cairngorms and Northern Highlands being the most visited. However, these are also the most 'serious' mountains and many of them will be out of reach of beginners.

A favourite book of mine is The UK's County Tops by Jonny Muir which details 82 walking routes to the highest points (tops) of each county in England, Wales, Scotland and Northern Ireland. If you're not lucky enough to live in the mountains then setting yourself the challenge of reaching the highest points in your local area is a great start.

What is the CRoW Act?

The Countryside and Rights of Way Act 2000, colloquially known as the 'Right to Roam', is an Act of Parliament affecting England and Wales (I'll explain Scotland's more relaxed stance later), which gives walkers permission to use open access land without the need to stick rigidly to public footpaths. This was a huge achievement by walking and outdoor organisations and is extremely valuable to those exploring the countryside.

Note that the law talks about 'walkers' – this is important as the rules don't extend to cyclists, horse riders or motorised vehicles, or to wild camping. Much of this land is privately owned and there's a fine balance to be upheld between free access and maintaining relationships with landowners.

The universal sign to indicate the start of CRoW or 'open access' land. You might see this on gates or fence posts when out and about in England and Wales.

It's estimated that around 865,000 hectares in England alone is classed as 'Open Access' land. Of course, many would like this to be even greater.

Open Access land can be identified on Ordnance Survey 1:25k Explorer maps by a yellow 'wash' with a thick orange border, which really makes the land stand out. Natural England and Natural Resources Wales maintain public databases of Open Access land, both of which are available online.

When you're out walking, you'll often (but not always) come across the brown circular CRoW sign, showing a walker on a hill as you enter Open Access land. This can also be a useful navigation aid if you're using a map.

The Scots went even further than the CRoW Act by introducing the Land Reform (Scotland) Act 2003, which essentially gives everyone unhindered access to the countryside for walking, cycling and wild camping. Of course, certain responsibilities come with these rights and it's vital that we all work together to protect them. For example, don't interfere with farming operations and if you're wild camping, leave the area exactly as you find it.

Finding route ideas

In your early mountain climbing days, there's little point re-inventing the wheel. Sorry if I'm shattering any illusions here but all the UK's mountains have already been climbed, and by people much more experienced than you or I. This does mean that there are a huge number of resources out there to make your life easier.

Starting with this book. At the back you'll find detailed route maps and guides to what I believe are some of our most popular and achievable hill and mountain walks. Every route is designed for beginners who may not have any more outdoor experience than simply reading this book. They mostly follow marked footpaths which should make for easy navigation and are all popular with walkers so it's unlikely you're ever going to be on your own.

The CRoW Act gives this group of experienced walkers the rights to explore away from the paths.

Guide books

There is a plethora of guide books available for mountain walking in the UK, aimed at all sorts of audiences. Try your local book shop or online retailer and search for 'walking guide books'. If you're planning to spend an extended amount of time in one particular area, you'll also find guide books covering popular national parks for example. Outdoor publishers such as Pesda Press (who publish this book), Cicerone and Cordee are all good places to start.

An example of a guide book aimed at those wanting to walk the Lake District's Wainwrights.

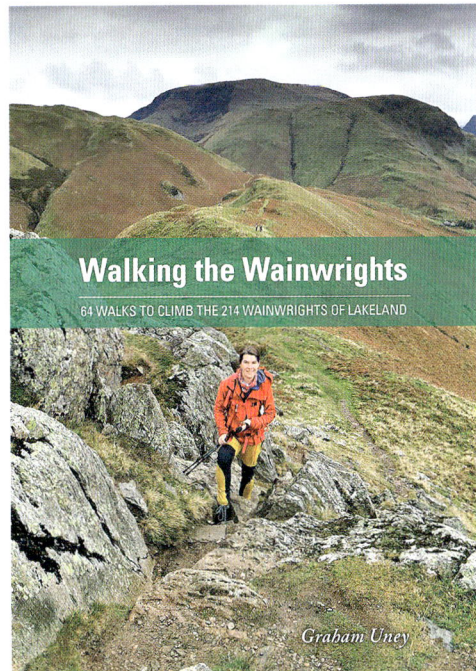

Walking the Wainwrights

64 WALKS TO CLIMB THE 214 WAINWRIGHTS OF LAKELAND

Graham Uney

Outdoor magazines

These are a great way to stay up to date with the latest developments in the outdoor world, as well as checking out the latest outdoor gear and for sourcing route ideas.

There are three popular titles in the UK that you'll find on most newsagent and supermarket shelves, and are often available free from your local library. Published monthly, they each focus on the outdoors and include a selection of walks of varying difficulties with detailed maps and route descriptions.

Country Walking magazine is described as the go-to companion for anyone who wants to discover a more beautiful Britain, and get happier and healthier, on foot. From spectacular views to hidden secrets, *Country Walking* will show you where to go, what to look for, and how to get more out of your passion.

Outdoor magazines

Trail Magazine – the UK's best-selling hill walking magazine is aimed at those looking to venture into the hills and mountains of the UK. It features independent gear reviews written by experienced industry experts, and route guides and destination-focused articles. These are written either by its staff or their trusted team of freelance contributors, many of them guidebook authors and all of them leading authorities in the outdoor industry.

The Great Outdoors calls itself the original mountain magazine and has been leading people to explore high places for more than 40 years. Through compelling writing, beautifully illustrated stories and eye-catching content, across a range of platforms, it seeks to convey the joy of adventure, the thrill of mountainous and wild environments, and the wonder of the natural world.

PressReader

Did you know you can read all these outdoor magazines and many more each month for free? All thanks to PressReader and your local library.

PressReader is an online resource where you can read thousands of newspapers and magazines from around the globe. Subscribers get access to more than 7,000 of the world's top publications as soon as they're available on shelves. But did you know that many UK libraries offer a PressReader subscription free with your library card? Simply sign up at pressreader.com, select your library, enter your library card number and hey presto, free access to all the outdoor magazines (and more!) that you could ever wish for all from the comfort of your own home.

Of course, if like me you love reading on the go, the PressReader app is the best way to read magazines and newspapers on your mobile phone or tablet. Download complete issues and toggle between the original print view and a mobile-optimised text view. You can bring your favourite outdoor publication to life with 'listening mode', one-touch translation and dynamic links.

Smartphone Apps

There is an ever-increasing number of smartphone apps available offering all sorts of mountain walking routes ideas. Popular options are AllTrails, FATMAP, Komoot, Outdooractive and the OSMaps app from Ordnance Survey. These all offer similar features, some of which are free but many require a paid subscription.

Apps usually include some form of mapping; however, this might be quite rudimentary and is unlikely to be of good quality. Premium (paid-for) app options will include Ordnance Survey or even Harvey mapping which is essential for effective and safe navigation. You'll also be able to track your mountain walk or follow other people's route suggestions. If you come up with your own awesome hike, you can share that with others and include a route description and photos.

An important warning about apps!

Unlike guide books and magazines which are written and published by professionals, walking routes found in apps can be uploaded by absolutely anybody. This can lead beginners into dangerous territory. Just because 'Dave from Bedford' has shared his favourite mountain hike and called it 'easy' doesn't necessarily mean anything.

There are frequent stories in the press about people getting lost, following 'apps'. They definitely have a place but with some caveats.

When searching for a mountain walk, look for 'approved', 'verified' or 'recommended' routes. These are typically reproduced from guide books or outdoor magazines so generally come with a level of authenticity.

Many apps also allow you to review routes, so read what others have written. If there are comments about people finding the instructions difficult to follow and getting lost, maybe try a different one.

Websites

There are a great selection of websites offering mountain walking route ideas. Typically compiled by individuals or small groups of people with an interest in a particular area, they're usually free to use but can be a bit 'ad-heavy'.

Some examples are *www.go4awalk.com*, *www.walkhighlands.co.uk*, *www.walkingbritain.co.uk* and *www.walkingworld.com*.

If you're interested in long distance walking, *www.nationaltrail.co.uk* provides detailed route guides about the 15 National Trails across England and Wales or *www.scotlandsgreattrails.com* for information about Scotland's 29 Great Trails.

Starting early in the morning to maximise your daylight hours.　　*Photo: Monkey Business Images, Dreamstime.com*

5　When to Go

If you're reading this book, I'm going to assume you're fairly new to walking in the countryside and certainly new to reaching mountain tops. Therefore, for these purposes, I'm really only going to talk about exploring the hills and mountains of the UK in spring, summer and autumn.

Mountains around the UK, and certainly those in England and Wales, are usually climbable in the three non-winter seasons; assuming you have what's called 'summer conditions' (which is pretty much summed up as 'no snow'). If there's snow on the ground at your starting point, or if it's forecast during your day, then that's not the right time for you to be out walking unless you're with a competent and experienced person.

You should normally be safe from around Easter until the end of October, but of course you should still check the ground conditions and weather forecast before you start. You can find out more about where to get a mountain specific weather forecast later in the book.

The mountains in winter

Winter walking is a very different ball game – The Cairngorms, Scotland.   *Photo: Alex Croall*

Climbing mountains in the winter, particularly when there is snow on the ground, requires a very different set of skills and brings with it much greater risk. You'll need extra equipment, such as crampons and an ice axe, and you'll need training on how to use them. You'll also need to be much fitter and something of an expert in navigation. So, for now, keep your mountain walking outside of the winter months.

Start early

When thinking about the best time of day to tackle your mountain walk, without doubt the best advice I can give is to **start early!** Particularly if you're looking to climb a popular mountain via a busy route over a summer weekend.

Yr Wyddfa (Snowdon), for example, is more fortunate than many other UK mountains in that it has lots of parking at its most popular starting points. However, on sunny summer weekends, many more people will want to hike to the summit than there is space for cars. This causes all sorts of problems for locals, who get angry when they can't park outside their own homes, and for visitors who risk having their cars towed away by the police, who regularly have to enforce measures against dangerous, illegal parking on narrow mountain passes.

Starting early in the day gives you the most daylight.
Photo: Val_th, Dreamstime.com

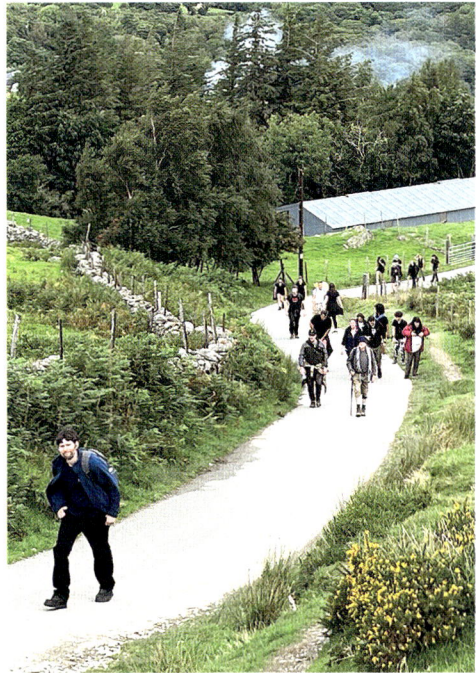

Starting later in the day might let you have a lie in but
also means you could be climbing with the crowds.

By setting off early in the morning you're much more likely to get a parking spot in one of the main car parks, and, more importantly, you have a better chance of a peaceful day out. National newspapers love to print photos of queues up to the summit of Yr Wyddfa (Snowdon) but, in reality, this only happens a few days each year, typically on summer Saturdays or bank holiday weekends, and is easily avoidable by getting yourself out of bed a bit earlier.

So, what do I mean by 'early'? If you know it's going to be a busy weekend then I'd recommend starting your walk before dawn. If you feel confident enough and have a headtorch and a good idea of where you're going, then setting off while it's still dark is even better – perhaps an hour or so before sunrise. However, there are greater risks associated with walking in the dark, so this should only be attempted by those who feel up for it.

You can find out what time the sun is going to rise on any particular day with an Internet search for 'Llanberis sunrise times' (for Yr Wyddfa (Snowdon) for example). Aim to be at the starting point with your boots on, ready to walk at about this time. Be aware though, that on very busy days this still might not be early enough.

A busy afternoon queuing on the summit of Yr Wyddfa (Snowdon).   *Photo: Tony Ellis*

It's also worth bearing in mind that the amount of daylight you'll have available to you will vary dramatically from the beginning of spring and end of autumn to the height of summer, also from northern Scotland down to the south of England. If you're out walking in England and Wales in summertime then you're unlikely to have an issue but if you wanted to tackle Ben Nevis in late autumn or early spring, you're not going to have enough daylight hours without starting in the dark.

Walk in the week

This is great advice particularly if you're heading to one of the more popular mountains. I closely monitor visitor numbers on Yr Wyddfa (Snowdon) each year for my day job, and the stats very clearly show Saturday is the busiest day of the week by a long way. There's quite a big drop-off then to Sunday and a huge drop in numbers on weekdays.

If you're planning a big mountain day, book some time off work and head up on a Wednesday instead of the weekend, and you're sure to have a much more enjoyable experience.

A quiet early morning on Yr Wyddfa (Snowdon).

Avoid bank holiday weekends and school holidays (if you possibly can)

When the whole country stops working on sunny bank holiday weekends, everyone heads to the mountains (or retail parks!) and this rarely makes for an enjoyable day out at either. Popular mountains will be inundated with extra visitors and your experience will be less than optimal. If you're planning on visiting busy areas and are not able to start early then you're likely to be in a procession of people marching up and down. Generally, the Saturday of a bank holiday weekend is the busiest day with the Sunday being quieter and the Monday typically being the quietest.

There is a similar effect during the school holidays (Easter, summer and half term breaks). Expect popular mountain locations to be considerably busier during these times, so if you're not walking with children, definitely try to avoid these dates.

Search gov.uk online for 'school term and holiday dates' for more information on times of the year to avoid.

If the weather deteriorates during your mountain day, it might be time for plan B.

Don't be afraid to change your plans

I often bump into people struggling up a mountain path through truly horrible conditions, and when I ask why they chose that particular day they usually answer with something like "It's been in the calendar for months". That's not a good reason. Check the weather, check the ground conditions, check your fitness, check you're ready. If you're not happy with all these then postpone your mountain day.

There's no reason why you can't climb a mountain in most conditions … but certainly in your early days you'll have a much more enjoyable day out if the conditions are right.

We should all do our bit to look after the countryside. *Photo: Jasminelove, Dreamstime.com*

6 The Countryside Code

Produced by Natural England on behalf of the UK Government and dating back to the 1930's, The Countryside Code is a set of 'rules' for visitors to follow when in the outdoors. I first remember learning about it in Cubs, but sadly it's still not part of the curriculum in schools, and many first-time visitors to the countryside have little or no awareness of it. I might be so bold as to suggest that much of it should be common sense. However, if you've spent most of your life growing up in a busy city you could be forgiven for not understanding some of the advice. The latest version of the code was released in April 2021, aimed at bringing it up to date and going someway to help deal with the many post-pandemic issues caused by the rapid increase in visitors.

The revised code can be neatly summed up into three messages: respect everyone, protect the environment and enjoy the outdoors. **Please** just take a few minutes to read it before venturing out into the hills for the first time, even if only just the summary shown here.

(The Scots have their own, much more in–depth version called the Outdoor Access Code which you'll be able to find online if you're planning to tackle a mountain in Scotland.)

The Countryside Code
NATURAL ENGLAND

Your guide to enjoying parks and waterways, coast and countryside

Respect everyone
- be considerate to those living in, working in and enjoying the countryside
- leave gates and property as you find them
- do not block access to gateways or driveways when parking
- be nice, say hello, share the space
- follow local signs and keep to marked paths unless wider access is available

Protect the environment
- take your litter home - leave no trace of your visit
- take care with BBQs and do not light fires
- always keep dogs under control and in sight
- dog poo - bag it and bin it - any public waste bin will do
- care for nature - do not cause damage or disturbance

Enjoy the outdoors
- check your route and local conditions
- plan your adventure - know what to expect and what you can do
- enjoy your visit, have fun, make a memory

Stay safe — FOLLOW SOCIAL DISTANCING

www.gov.uk/countryside-code

The Countryside Code
NATURAL ENGLAND

Follow advice and local signs
In some cases, additional higher rights of access or permissive access could exist.

Footpath | Bridleway

Restricted Byway | Byway open to all traffic

Permissive Path
Follow advice on local signs as landowners voluntarily provide access to these paths and choose who can use them. Some open access areas are also made available in the same way.

National Trail
National Trails are created for walking, with horse-riding and cycling possible on some trails or trail sections.
www.nationaltrail.co.uk

Open Access
You can walk and explore away from paths.
www.openaccess.naturalengland.org.uk

For further information visit www.gov.uk/countryside-code

Respect everyone

- Be considerate to those living in, working in and enjoying the countryside.

- Leave gates and property as you find them.

- Do not block access to gateways or driveways when parking.

- Be nice, say hello, share the space.

- Follow local signs and keep to marked paths unless wider access is available.

Farming, livestock and wild animals

Your actions can affect other people's lives and livelihoods.

Co-operate with people working in the countryside. For example, follow the farmer's directions when animals are being moved or gathered. This helps keep everybody safe.

Leave gates and property as you find them or follow instructions on signs. When in a group, make sure the last person knows how to leave the gates. Farmers close gates to keep animals in or leave them open to give access to food and water. Do not interfere with farm machinery, horses or livestock. If you think a farm animal is in distress, try to alert the farmer.

Give wild animals, livestock and horses plenty of space. Their behaviour can be unpredictable, especially when they are with their young, and you could get hurt.

Do not feed livestock, horses or wild animals as it can cause them harm.

Travel and parking in the countryside

Traffic on country roads can be dangerous to people and wildlife.

Slow down and drive carefully on rural roads. Make sure you do not block access to gateways or driveways when parking. Always leave access for emergency vehicles.

Consider leaving your car at home when visiting the outdoors. You could use public transport instead. Find public transport information on the Traveline website.

Take extra care and stay alert where a right of way crosses a railway line. You can find guidance on safely using level crossings on the Network Rail website.

Face oncoming traffic and follow The Highway Code when you walk on a road without a pavement.

Be nice, say hello, share the space

When you're spending time outdoors you could come across other users and animals. Slow down or stop for horses, walkers and livestock when driving or cycling. Always give them plenty of room.

Cyclists must give way to walkers and horse riders on bridleways.

Cyclists and horse riders should respect walkers' safety, but walkers should also take care not to obstruct or endanger them.

Follow local signs and keep to marked paths

Use maps and local signs to help you find your way. Stay on marked paths, even if they're muddy, unless wider access is available, such as on Open Access land. This helps to protect crops and wildlife.

A group of walkers enjoying the countryside responsibly.

Get to know the signs and symbols used in the countryside. They help you identify routes for different users through the countryside.

Use gates, stiles or gaps in field boundaries where you can. Climbing over boundaries can cause damage and put livestock at risk.

Contact the local authority if you think a sign is illegal or misleading. For example, a 'private – no entry' sign on a public footpath.

Protect the environment

- Take your litter home – leave no trace of your visit.

- Take care with BBQs and do not light fires.

- Always keep dogs under control and in sight.

- Dog poo – bag it and bin it – any public waste bin will do.

- Care for nature – do not cause damage or disturbance.

We all have a responsibility to protect our countryside and open spaces for current and future generations.

Care for nature – do not cause damage or disturbance. Leave rocks, stones, plants and trees as you find them and take care not to disturb wildlife, including birds that nest on the ground.

Do not disturb ruins or historic sites – our heritage in the natural and built environment is important.

Take your litter home – leave no trace of your visit

Remember to bring a bag with you and take your rubbish and food waste home. Use public bins or recycle if possible. Litter spoils the beauty of the countryside and can be dangerous to wildlife and livestock. Dropping litter and dumping rubbish are criminal offences.

Take care with BBQs and do not light fires

Be careful with naked flames and cigarettes. Only use BBQs where signs state they are allowed. Always put your BBQ out, make sure the ashes are cold and dispose of them responsibly. Fires can be as devastating to wildlife and habitats as they are to people and property.

Controlled fires are used by some land managers to manage vegetation, particularly on heaths and moors between 1 October and 15 April. Call 999 if you see an unattended fire.

Always keep dogs under control and in sight

The countryside, parks and the coast are great places to exercise your dog but you need to consider other users and wildlife.

Keep your dog under effective control to make sure it stays away from wildlife, livestock, horses and other people unless invited. You should:

- Always keep your dog on a lead or in sight.

- Be confident your dog will return on command.

- Make sure your dog does not stray from the path or area where you have right of access.

Always check local signs, as there are situations when you must keep your dog on a lead for all or part of the year. Local areas may also ban dogs completely, except assistance dogs. Signs will tell you about these local restrictions.

It is good practice, wherever you are, to keep your dog on a lead around livestock.

On Open Access land and at the coast, you must put your dog on a lead around livestock. Between 1 March and 31 July, you must have your dog on a lead on open access land, even if there is no livestock on the land. These are legal requirements.

A farmer can shoot a dog that is attacking or chasing livestock. They may not be liable to compensate the dog's owner.

Let your dog off the lead if you feel threatened by livestock or horses. Do not risk getting hurt protecting your dog. Releasing your dog will make it easier for you both to reach safety.

Dog poo – bag it and bin it – any public waste bin will do

Always clean up your dog's poo because it can cause illness in people, livestock and wildlife.

Never leave bags of dog poo around, even if you intend to pick them up later. Deodorised bags and containers can make bags of dog poo easier to carry. If you cannot find a public waste bin, you should take it home and use your own bin.

Enjoy the outdoors

- Check your route and local conditions.

- Plan your adventure – know what to expect and what you can do.

- Enjoy your visit, have fun, make a memory.

The outdoors is great for your wellbeing. It is a place for relaxation, peacefulness and activity. Whatever you like to do outdoors, you will enjoy it more if you prepare in advance.

Check your route and local conditions

Make sure you know your route and have the maps you need. Refer to up to date maps, guides or websites before you set off.

You can find advice on specialist activities from outdoor recreation groups. Websites such as GetOutside, Visit England or Visit Britain can provide a list of these groups. Information centres can also give you local ideas and advice.

Check weather, tide and water conditions

Check weather forecasts before you set off. Conditions can change quickly on mountains and along the coast. Do not be afraid to turn back if conditions change when you're out and about.

Look up tide times before you leave to reduce the risk of getting cut off by rising tides. Some rivers are affected by tidal change, it's not just the sea. Take care on slippery rocks and seaweed.

Check the Environment Agency website for water quality and conditions if you want to paddle, swim or enjoy the water.

Plan your adventure – know what to expect and what you can do

Tell someone else where you are going and when you expect to be back. In rural areas you may not see anyone for hours and phone signals are unreliable in many places.

You are responsible for the safety of yourself, and others in your care. Make sure you have the skills and knowledge you need for your activity.

Prepare for natural hazards, including weather changes, to stay safe. Make sure you take the right clothing and equipment for your planned activities.

Remain flexible in case you need to change your plans if places are busy.

Rights and permissions

This code sets out information about the rights of different users. For some activities you may need to get permission from the landowner, including:

- camping

- freshwater swimming

- freshwater fishing

Know the signs and symbols of the countryside

In some cases, additional, broader rights of access or permissive access could exist.

A yellow arrow – footpath, a right of way for walkers and mobility aid users.

A blue arrow – bridleway, a right of way for walkers, mobility aid users, horse riders and cyclists.

A purple arrow – restricted byway, a right of way for walkers, mobility aid users, cyclists, horse riders and horse-drawn vehicles only.

A red arrow – byway open to all traffic, a right of way for all users including motorised vehicles.

An acorn symbol – National Trail, created for walking, with horse riding and cycling possible on some trails. Users with limited mobility can visit the National Trail website to check trail suitability. This website also contains maps, trip planning tools and information on trail diversions. This symbol marks 16 long distance routes in England and Wales, including the England Coast Path.

Round brown symbol with a person walking over hills – Open Access, you can explore away from paths. This includes many areas of mountain, moorland, heath, down, coastal margin, registered common land. Check the Open Access website for maps, information and any access restrictions.

A local sign on a post or gate – permissive path. Follow advice on local signs as landowners voluntarily provide access to these paths and choose who can use them. Some Open Access areas are also made available in the same way.

Be AdventureSmart. If you can't answer yes to the three questions, choose another day.

AdventureSmart

AdventureSmart is the outdoor safety campaign with a very simple message; ask yourself three questions before you set off:

- Do I have the right gear?

- Do I know what the weather will be like?

- Am I confident I have the knowledge and skills for the day?

Do I have the right gear?

If this question prompts you to ask, 'what is the right gear?' then you need help. Outdoor kit doesn't need to be expensive but does need to keep you warm and dry. In the case of boots, they need to fit well as there is nothing like a blister to ruin a good day's walking.

Do I know what the weather will be like?

As we know, the weather has the potential to make or spoil your day. This doesn't have to mean that a spot of drizzle or even a howling gale has to stop us in our tracks. Like a good Scout, being prepared and adapting your plans is the key to being in control of your day. Check the weather forecast – the Met Office is a good place to start.

Am I confident I have the knowledge & skills for the day?

Adventure allows us to step outside our comfort zone and is a great way to discover a zest for life. Being AdventureSmart simply means thinking about your own experience and skills. Choosing an adventure that you know is within your skill set is part of the fun. If you want to do something that pushes beyond this, there are many ways to find a guide or instructor to help you.

#BeAdventureSmart

Heading for the hills? #BeAdventureSmart
Ask yourself 3 questions...

1. Am I confident I have the KNOWLEDGE AND SKILLS for the day?
- Plan for a great day: Know where you are going
- Know your limits: Be honest with yourself about your and your companions' knowledge, fitness
- Let the experts show you the way: Go with a qualified guide or sign up for some training

2. Do I know what the WEATHER will be like?
- Watch the weather: Check the latest weather and ground conditions for your destination, go to www.metoffice.gov.uk
- Only attempt a route if the conditions are within

3. Do I have the right GEAR?
- The right gear's a good idea: Stay warm and dry; wear walking boots and pack warm layers and waterproofs. Carry a map & compass and a charged mobile phone (but don't rely on it for navigation)

ADVENTURE SMART UK

Make your good day better
www.adventuresmart.uk

From its initial start in Wales in 2017, AdventureSmart launched UK-wide in 2019. AdventureSmart.UK is a positive strategy that encourages participation in the safe enjoyment of outdoor recreation with the aim of reducing the number of avoidable incidents that the rescue and emergency services deal with each year. Experts from leading safety and sporting organisations have developed these messages to provide all the essential information needed for people to get outdoors, confident that they have prepared for a great day.

Of course, as a result of reading this book you're already becoming 'Adventure Smart'!

Being well prepared for a mountain day increases your chances of enjoying it.   Photo: Dan Bannister, Dreamstime.com

7 What to Wear

What you should wear on a mountain day is probably the question I get asked the most. That's because getting it wrong can, at best, spoil your day, and in the worst-case scenario, lead to much worse – but it's really not that difficult if you follow a few simple rules.

There's no need to spend a fortune on high-end outdoor clothing. You'll see people out in the mountains wearing waterproof jackets that cost £400+, and they are really good if you're going to be spending day after day outdoors in the rain. For most people, the raincoat you've got in the cupboard will do just fine, certainly in your early mountain walking days.

One of the best tips I can give is to visit your local outdoor shop. Whether it's a little independent store in your local town or a large chain such as Go Outdoors, the staff will be well used to people asking questions about what they need for the outdoors. So don't be afraid to ask.

Test out your gear before you really need it. Don't try out those new boots on a big mountain day. Give them a run-in around the neighbourhood first.

A good pair of well looked after walking boots should last you years.

Let's start from the bottom.

Feet

You'll need something comfy to walk in. Exactly what they are will depend on which mountain you're going to be climbing, how long you think it's going to take you, and how much money you have. Very simply, hiking boots are better than walking shoes and walking shoes are better than trainers. That's not to say that if you've got a good pair of sturdy trainers, you won't enjoy yourself on an easy day out in fine weather. You might just end up with a blister after a while, and soggy feet if it rains. For shorter, easy walks over good terrain, there's nothing wrong with walking in a comfortable pair of trainers, but when you start venturing out on longer days and over rockier ground or in poor weather conditions, you're going to want something sturdier that's able to provide protection for your feet and ankles.

Walking shoes look like a pair of trainers except they'll have a stiffer sole with good grip, will often be waterproof to some degree (a key requirement in my books) and typically be made of fabric. These really come into their own over a standard pair of trainers when covering longer distances and on rocky ground. A day out will often start on nice, tarmacked tracks but will quickly turn in to a rocky path. Walking shoes will give you better grip over this sort of ground.

Hiking boots are similar to walking shoes in that they will have a sturdy sole and give you excellent grip. They have the added benefit of ankle protection, which is essential when you start taking on even rougher mountain paths such as on Scafell Pike or Ben Nevis. They're available in fabric or leather, and in all sorts of designs.

If you're planning to do more than a couple of day's mountain walking then I'd strongly recommend investing in a sturdy pair of hiking boots. They don't have to be expensive. If you're not sure which ones to choose, the staff at your local outdoor shop will be able to offer advice and even fit them for you. Aim for something with ankle support to get the best protection. Boots made from leather will tend to be longer lasting and more waterproof than fabric ones, but they will need a bit more caring for and are likely to be a bit heavier and more expensive.

As with all outdoor gear, think about what you're going to be using it for. If you only really plan on getting outside during summer weekends then you probably don't need top end winter boots. If you're planning to commit to mountain walking as a hobby, my advice is to aim for something in the middle. A nice waterproof walking boot will keep your feet warm and dry all day long and, if looked after, will last for many years.

I love shopping online as much as the next young and trendy bloke and there isn't anything you can't buy over the Internet these days. However, walking boots are one of those items that are best bought in person from a good outdoor shop. The staff are often 'outdoorsy' people themselves and will be well trained in making sure you get the right boot for your needs.

Try out your walking boots before your big mountain day.

When you go shopping for footwear, take your walking socks with you or borrow a pair from the shop as they'll be thicker than your normal day-to-day socks. When you get your boots home it's important to wear them a few times around the house or on short, local walks before a big mountain day, to 'wear them in' and to make sure they're a good fit. If something's not quite right, it's better to find out round the corner from your home rather than halfway up a mountain. Many outdoor shops will let you try them at home for a short time to make sure they're comfortable.

Still looking after your feet, socks are important too. Depending on your commitment, a good pair of sports socks will often do just fine. There's a bewildering variety of walking socks available made of all sorts of materials with a wide range of price points. This is really down to personal preference. I've got naturally warm feet, so with my nice pair of leather walking boots I tend to wear lightweight walking socks. The half-dozen or so pairs I currently own have lasted me nearly a decade, and they weren't expensive ones. I also have much thicker socks I wear when I'm out in winter conditions but it really has to be very cold for me to need them. Decide yourself on what your feet are like. You're probably only going to need one pair of walking socks and warm feet can make your mountain day – so get yourself a good pair.

Avoid wearing more than one pair of socks at a time as the friction can lead to blisters. It's better to have one pair of good socks than a couple of pairs of rubbish ones. If you're out on a particularly long day, pack a spare pair of socks in your rucksack in case the ones you're wearing get wet, or just to give you a fresh feel for the way down.

Bottoms

Walking trousers are durable and lightweight, and provide excellent protection against the elements. The more you get out in to the countryside, the more different environments you're going to experience. You can soon find yourself rubbing up against rock or vegetation or walking through long grass, so a decent pair of dedicated walking trousers will go a long way to protecting your legs and should last you a good while.

I do like the 'convertible' ones where you can zip off the bottom part to turn them in to a pair of shorts, as this gives you choices if the weather changes and means you don't need to buy a separate pair of walking shorts. Another zip up the sides makes it easy for them to come off without the need to remove footwear. Good walking trousers don't have to be expensive and will make a real difference to your day.

If you're just starting out, only doing short, easy walks and if you're absolutely certain of the weather, then tracksuit bottoms or leggings (or shorts on sunny days) will do the job. However, bear in mind that they won't do much to protect your legs from scuffs and injury, nor are they very good in wet conditions. Jeans are a definite no for a mountain day as, when they get wet, they become heavy and cold and are slow to dry.

Waterproof overtrousers are another essential investment for when you start climbing bigger mountains, spend longer outdoors or know you're going to be walking in the rain. Your walking trousers are unlikely to be waterproof so overtrousers that pull on easily over your trousers will keep the rain off and also provide an extra layer of warmth. More expensive options will have side zips that make it easy for you to put them on and take them off even when you're wearing a big pair of walking boots. There's not much to them, so they fold away nicely and won't take up a lot of room in your rucksack. You can pick up a pair for as little as a tenner and they'll make a world of difference on a rainy day.

It's worth taking time to think about your underwear too. Your day-to-day undies are typically going to be made of cotton which doesn't perform well during activity as it absorbs sweat and will become heavy, cold and slow to dry (and smelly too!). As with everything else, if you're starting out with small, easy walks, then they'll be fine, so just make sure whatever you're wearing is comfortable. But as you begin

A well dressed hill walker

to progress to longer and tougher mountain days, investing in a pair of good 'active' underwear will make things a lot nicer 'down there'.

The properties you're looking for are breathability, moisture-wicking and quick-drying. Moisture-wicking is an amazing technology that 'wicks' away sweat from the body without making the garment wet and because they don't hold the sweat they don't smell, so when you progress to multi-day expeditions you can wear the same pair of underwear for days on end! A good pair of 'sports' or 'active' underwear will do all this, with materials like merino wool and bamboo being good options to look for.

If you're particularly susceptible to the cold or for when you start moving into winter walking, you might also want to look into thermal leggings or long johns. I rarely get that cold as to need this level of insulation, and find a good pair of winter walking trousers with waterproof overtrousers will provide all the warmth I need.

Top

The key to your top half is layers, as when you're climbing a mountain you want options. The air temperature you start out with will be very different to the air temperature at the top of the mountain and you're going to feel warmer walking uphill than you will coming down, so you want to be able to easily add or remove layers during your day. We can break these layers down into three types: base layers, mid layers and outer layers.

Base layer

This is the layer that's closest to your skin. At the height of summer and on an easy, low-level walk this might be the only layer you wear. Just like your underwear choice, a material that can wick moisture away from the skin is going to be best and will help you maintain a comfortable body temperature, so look out for tops made from materials such as synthetics or merino wool. These will keep you warm in the winter and cool in the summer. Conversely, cotton will tend to hold the moisture which will become cold and uncomfortable.

Available as short or long sleeved and for as little as a few pounds, there are a huge choice of options available. They don't have to be 'walking' tops either. The same moisture-wicking technology is used in lots of 'active wear'. I regularly interchange my running, watersports and hiking tops. Above all, make sure you have something that's comfortable.

Mid layer

Next up is your mid layer. This is something you put on over your moisture wicking base layer and underneath your jacket, and it is typically a fleece of some sort. The job of the mid layer is to provide warmth. They're available in all sorts of designs and made from lots of different materials. Look for something that fits well, is comfortable, warm and looks good! Most will pack away nicely in your rucksack and don't mind being crumpled up.

I have a variety of fleeces that I like to wear for different days out. I've got a couple of really nice warm ones that I can only really wear in winter. A couple more have thumb loops at the wrists, which are great for extending the sleeves over your hands for extra protection and added warmth. Another couple have built in face coverings in the hoods, which means I can quickly and easily cover my face when the wind picks up and the temperature plummets.

Outer layer

Your final layer is the outer layer which is what protects you from the weather. Critical to any day out in the UK is a waterproof jacket. Even if the sun's cracking the flagstones

Being well dressed with the right outdoor gear enables you to cope with any conditions.

as you set off and the forecast is looking tropical all day, you never know when the British weather is going to turn. They don't take up much space in your rucksack and are a great extra layer for the summit if it turns cold or windy.

Buying a waterproof jacket can be a bit of a minefield. It's likely to be your most expensive piece of gear and typically has the widest price range. As with all outdoor gear, you need to decide what you want from it. If you're going to be bimbling around smaller mountains on the odd weekend over the summer, you'll be fine with an entry-level waterproof that could cost as little as £50. If you're planning ahead to more serious mountain days where you could be out in all conditions, you'll want to spend a bit more. I typically pay £300-£400 for my waterproof jackets but I'm frequently out day after day, and I know they will keep me dry even in the heaviest of rain, plus they usually last me at least a decade or longer.

This is definitely something I'd recommend chatting to the team at your local outdoor shop about. You'll be able to tell them what you plan to do and they'll be able to recommend options based on your budget.

You might also want an extra warm outer layer such as a synthetic or down jacket. I tend to keep one in a dry bag in my rucksack 'just in case' as they squash quite nicely.

However, I rarely wear it outside of winter as my other layers are usually sufficient. If you're planning a sunrise walk or if it's a very cold day, it's a useful extra layer.

Some of the author's collection of mountain hats and gloves (while it would appear hats can be bright and eye-catching, gloves seemingly only come in one colour!).

Hats and gloves

Don't neglect your extremities! It will be much colder at the top of the mountain than when you start out, so be sure to have a warm hat and a good pair of gloves. I regularly pack two hats and a couple of different types of gloves. A thinnish pair that are great for lower temperatures and a thick, winter pair for when it gets really cold.

I've never found a pair of truly waterproof gloves so the only answer you have here is to carry multiple pairs. In winter, I'll typically carry three or four pairs of gloves in my rucksack.

Outdoor retailers

You can buy outdoor gear from all sorts of places and each have their pros and cons. When starting out there's nothing wrong with the large chains like Go Outdoors or Decathlon. They have vast stores with a wide range of entry-level products at entry-level prices. They're usually staffed by people with an interest in the outdoors but perhaps not by outdoor experts.

Then you have what you might call your 'expert' outdoor shops such as Cotswold Outdoor or Tiso in Scotland, where you'll possibly pay more but should expect better, more professional service. These retailers pride themselves on having staff that know and love the outdoors. They'll stock higher-end brands and professional gear.

If you're lucky enough to live near the mountains, you'll also have access to a selection of independent outdoor retailers. The Climbers Shop / Joe Brown's and Cunninghams are just a couple of examples. Here you'll likely pay the most (although deals / discounts are often available) but you're certain of excellent service. All the independent shops around where I live are staffed by current or former outdoor professionals, and there isn't anything they don't know about climbing mountains (and they'll love telling you about it!).

A little tip – you should rarely have to pay full price at most outdoor retailers as they offer discounts for all sorts of organisations. If you're planning to spend big money on new outdoor gear and you're not already eligible for a discount, join the British Mountaineering Council for around £30 and you'll typically get 10-15% off at most retailers in store and online.

Be prepared. (I assume this charity walker had his waterproofs in his bag!)

Be bold – start cold!

A great mantra for mountain walking. When I'm guiding members of the public up mountains, they frequently rock up to the meeting point wearing everything I've told them to bring with them. They then start stripping off after a few minutes of uphill walking.

Get in the habit of losing the layers before you start. Your body will naturally warm up as you move, particularly if you're straight in to climbing.

MountainXperience
EXPLORE • CHALLENGE • LEARN

Mountain Day Kit List

Our kit list is aimed at those new to mountain walking who might be venturing out on their first mountain day. It's not an exhaustive list and you might find you need some extra things not shown here. A more thorough guide is available online at mountainxperience.uk and advice can always be sought from our mountain guides.

☐ Rucksack	☐ Woolly hat/sun hat
☐ Walking shoes/boots	☐ Gloves
☐ Warm socks (plus a spare pair in your rucksack)	☐ Gaiters
☐ Walking Trousers	☐ Dry bags/bin liners to keep things dry
☐ Waterproof Overtrousers	☐ Walking Poles
☐ Wicking Underwear	☐ Food - enough to last you all day plus spare
☐ Base Layer (eg a t-shirt)	☐ Water - at least one litre preferably double that
☐ Mid layer such as a fleece (plus a spare in your rucksack)	☐ Personal first aid kit including any regular medications
☐ Outer layer (eg a lightweight jacket)	☐ Suncream
☐ Waterproof Jacket	☐ Head torch
☐ Some spare clothing items for emergencies	☐ Fully charged mobile phone

An example of a kit list, with useful tick boxes so you don't forget anything.

8 What to Take with You

We've discussed what you need to wear when climbing a mountain, but there's potentially a whole host of other stuff you're going to need to take with you. Much of this will depend on the nature of your mountain day but the following should provide a useful guide.

Rucksack

If nothing else, you're going to need something to carry your lunch in, so a rucksack is best here. There's no need for a huge expedition-size backpack if you're only planning a short hike. You just need something big enough to take what you need with you for your day out. This might take a bit of trial and error, but most outdoor shops sell 'day packs' designed just for this use. I regularly carry a 30-litre rucksack which is perfect for everything I need plus extra group bits, so this is a good size to aim for if you're walking as a family. You can even look at something a bit smaller if you'll be walking on your own, although I wouldn't go much smaller than 20 litres.

Your rucksack will be on your back all day long, so choosing wisely here can make a big difference. If you're going to progress into more serious mountain walking, I'd recommend buying in person from a good outdoor shop. You'll be able to look at lots of

A well-fitted rucksack is essential for a happy mountain day. Colour coordination is a bonus!

different packs and try them on to see how they feel. The staff will also be able to advise you on fitting (having a correctly fitted rucksack can make a huge difference to your day out). Models with back netting are also great for ventilation – keeping the canvas of your rucksack away from your body and stopping you from getting a sweaty back.

Many brands also offer women's-fit rucksacks, which have a more rounded shape with higher hip straps.

Something to bear in mind is that most rucksacks aren't waterproof. If yours doesn't come with a rain cover (a pull-out waterproof cover usually found in a small zip pocket at the base of your bag), you'll need something inside to keep your gear dry. Experienced mountain walkers use dry bags so they can sort the contents of their rucksacks, but a big, strong black bin liner or a couple of good quality plastic carrier bags rolled over several times at the top will also do the job.

Walking poles

The single most useful way to protect your knees, particularly on your way down a mountain, is by using a pair of walking poles. Available in all sorts of styles and with many different 'features', they can cost as little as £20 for a pair that are perfectly adequate for most, to nearly £200 for super light, spring-loaded carbon poles.

They nearly all 'fold' away somehow, usually into themselves, so that when storing or transporting they'll be half or a third of their 'extended' length. The more expensive models will have clips and fancy mechanisms, the cheaper options are more likely to seize up, particularly if left stored for long periods in the garage.

Walking poles are really simple to use. Extend the poles so you have a 90° angle at your elbow, put your hand through the wrist strap so that it sits between your thumb and the palm of your hand and maintain a relaxed grip. When going downhill you can lengthen the poles slightly and when going uphill you can shorten them, but there's no need to spend too much time faffing around – just do what feels comfortable.

Walking poles can be a lifesaver for tired legs.
Photo: Antonio Guillem, Dreamstime.com

If you're worried about your knees, sometimes suffer from 'jelly legs', or have balance issues, then give them a go. It's essential, like so many other points here, that you try them out before your big mountain day. You need to know how to assemble them and be comfortable using them.

I'm in two minds about the day-to-day use of walking poles. I started using them regularly in my mid 30's but found I was becoming almost too reliant on them. While they did make me feel more confident, particularly on long mountain descents, I began to wonder if I was just moving the issue somewhere else. I now hardly ever use them (other than using a single pole in winter conditions) and feel much better. But that's my story and we all have different knees.

Gaiters

These may not be the coolest accessories and they really only come into their own in the rain, on the muddiest of walks, when crossing streams or when out in the snow – but if you are walking in any of those conditions, you'll thank me for having a pair. Gaiters (often called ankle gaiters) are water and windproof 'covers' for the top of your boots, ankles and lower legs that secure with a strap around the in-step of your

Gaiters   *Photo: Andreaobzerova, Dreamstime.com*

boot and tighten above the calf with an adjustable cord. They may have a small hook at the front which you pull over your laces to provide further protection and even more secure fitting. Gaiters usually have a zip or Velcro up the sides to make putting on and taking off easy, even if you're wearing big walking boots.

If it's raining or you're walking through a stream, gaiters help to reduce water getting into the top of your boots. If it's muddy, they'll keep the mud off your trousers, and if you're out in the snow, they'll stop the white stuff getting into your boots and also provide a welcome extra layer of warmth. They offer protection for your, perhaps expensive, walking trousers, which is particularly useful when winter walking with crampons. (I've put holes in many a pair of gaiters this way but I'd rather that than ruining my pricey winter walking trousers.) There isn't much to them either, so they pack away nicely and take up hardly any space in your rucksack.

Don't bother with the ankle-length, shorter variety; instead go for the full-length, much more useful option. Unless you're planning on lots of wet or winter walking, there's not really a lot to be gained by splashing out on big brand names. You should be able to pick up a pair for under a tenner.

If it's a really miserable day and you're wearing waterproof trousers, maintain the layering system by wearing your gaiters on top of your walking trousers but beneath your waterproof overtrousers. Wearing them as an outer layer means water will run down your trouser legs and in to the top of your gaiters, no matter how tight your pull the upper cord.

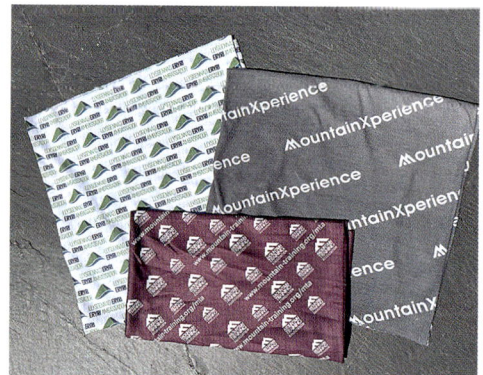

A selection of face coverings (sometimes called Buffs).

Whether it's your smartphone, compact, or DSLR camera, don't forget to take photos on your mountain day.

Face covering / BUFF®

Becoming more mainstream after the pandemic, mountain folk have been wearing face coverings for years. Sometimes referred to as snoods, face scarves or 'Buffs' (BUFF being a popular brand name), they're now available in all sorts of colours and styles, and from a huge variety of outlets.

They're a great way to protect your face from the elements in poor weather. BUFF advertise 12 ways to wear it, from face covering to headband to balaclava and more.

Camera

You want to be able to remember your big day, don't you? While your smartphone will take pretty good photos, those with a serious passion for photography might like to take along something a bit more professional. Make sure your battery is fully charged and I'd recommend a good carry case for protection. If you have a bulky SLR-type camera and a fancy lens, be aware of the added weight, which can be quite considerable over a long mountain day. I'm also wary of carrying them around your neck for extended periods of time. The 'dangling' can be distracting and, if you were to trip, the damage could be irreparable.

Tissues

Those little handy packs of tissues are indeed very handy and I always carry a couple of packs in my rucksack. Not just for snotty noses; they're a good substitute for toilet paper if the need arises and can help with some minor first aid too. Please take used tissues away with you; they're one of the most common items of litter found on the mountain.

Antibacterial hand sanitiser

Since we first learnt about COVID-19 we've all improved our hand hygiene (one good thing to come out of that horrible ordeal). Even before the pandemic, I would always have a 'travel' bottle of anti-bac in my rucksack to use before eating, but it's also handy for any time you need to clean your hands. Just think; how many people have touched that gate or stile before you?

Map

Depending on where you're going and what sort of day you're expecting, it could be useful to take a map with you. If you're going on an easy walk, perhaps using one of the routes in the back of this book, the map that comes with it will usually be sufficient; but as you develop and start venturing out onto bigger walks in more remote areas, carrying a good quality map becomes essential.

If you have a map, you need to be able to read it, so a map by itself is probably not much use. Later in the book I'll talk more about the different types of map available and give you a basic introduction to navigation in the hills.

Mobile phone

Just as you probably wouldn't leave home without your phone, you shouldn't be climbing a mountain without one either. As well as being an essential safety device, there are so many other benefits to carrying a mobile phone.

Safety – Being able to call for help if something goes wrong is the obvious reason for having your phone with you. Mobile phone signal is surprisingly good throughout the UK countryside, and even on top of mountains. Signal strength will vary greatly, depending on your mobile network and device, but for the sort of walks you're going to be doing as a beginner, it would be unusual for you to be out of mobile range for any extended period of time.

A map (and the skills to read one) should be something you have with you when exploring the mountains.

Smartphone Apps – Assuming you're not rocking a turn-of-the-century Nokia, most people today have a smartphone with the capability to download apps, of which there are a plethora that are useful in the outdoors. There are apps that can pinpoint your exact location, mapping apps to guide your route, and even 'virtual reality' apps that will identify mountains or plants just by pointing your phone at them. I've chosen not to list apps here as they change so frequently, but spend a bit of time before your mountain day seeing what you can find in your device's app store.

Camera – For most of us, gone are the days of having to carry a big expensive camera around, as even the most average smartphone can take amazing quality photos.

If you're worried about being bothered by the office when you're relaxing in the mountains, switch your phone to airplane mode which has the added advantage of extending your battery life.

Keeping your device safe is another thing to think about as most phones don't like getting wet. There are all sorts of water and weather proof cases available and if you're planning on spending lots of time in the outdoors, they're a wise investment. However, you can't really go wrong with a ziplock sandwich bag!

The most important thing to remember, is to charge your phone fully before heading out on your mountain day. I wouldn't even dream of starting a mountain walk without a full battery. Particularly in very cold weather, or if you're using navigation apps, you'll find your phone's battery will drain much quicker. Which leads me on to …

Mobile phone power bank

These are essentially just 'spare batteries' for your mobile phone. They're compact, light and can be a godsend on long days or overnight expeditions. You'll find them in all good electrical stores or online, starting from under a tenner and ranging from tiny things the size of a matchbox that might provide one full charge, to something that's a similar size to your mobile phone that can fully charge it multiple times.

I have a couple of these devices depending on the sort of day out I'm expecting – but of course, it's essential to remember to charge them too.

You may see people with mini solar panels strapped to the top of their rucksacks. I don't personally rate these as they're generally not hugely effective, as they're unlikely to be large enough to get a decent charge into a device.

Headtorch

A headtorch is also a valuable accessory to have with you, particularly if you're starting out before dawn or if you're walking in autumn / winter when the nights are drawing in. They're inexpensive, don't take up a lot of room in your rucksack, and can be lifesaver if you find yourself benighted (still outdoors after dark).

Personal first aid kit

There's no need to pack the family first aid tin from the kitchen, but having any regular medications, plasters, wipes and a few other things you might find useful is definitely worthwhile. As a contact lens wearer, I always carry a couple of spares too, as not being able to see would really spoil my day.

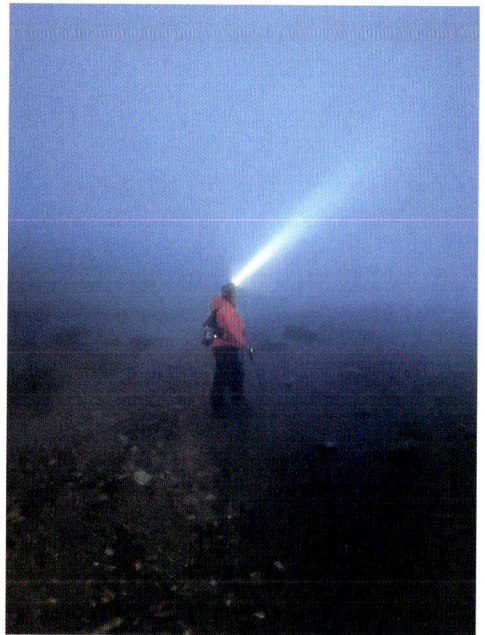

A headtorch is an essential item for any mountain day.
Photo: Tom Swinhoe

Make sure you pack plenty of snacks and drinks.   Photo: Peter Černič, Dreamstime.com

Your personal first aid kit should be just that, personal. It should be full of things that are useful to you.

Food and drink

Keeping yourself fuelled during your mountain day is essential, as is choosing the right foods. Big mountain days rarely offer the chance to sit down and have a picnic lunch at the summit. It's far more likely that you'll have multiple, shorter stops throughout the day, so think snacks rather than lunch platters.

Begin the day with a good breakfast. People often tell me that they don't usually eat breakfast as they start waning after a couple of hours, and my response is typically "you don't normally climb mountains". Even if it's 6 o'clock in the morning, if you're planning a big mountain day it's vital that you have something to eat. Porridge and similar slow-release breakfast foods are great.

Pack a variety of snacks. Some healthy bits, but some sugary stuff too. Nothing's going to give you a better boost than a chocolate bar or handful of Jelly Babies. Incidentally, Jelly Babies are the food of mountaineers! They're easy to carry, full of sugar and won't freeze in winter conditions.

Always remember to pack more food than you think you'll need. If you come off the mountain and you've consumed everything you packed, ask yourself what you would have done if something had gone wrong and your day turned out to be longer than planned?

Bring plenty of liquids for your day out. A litre of water per person really is the absolute minimum. If it's a hot day, I'd double or triple that. If it's a really cold day I'd also be carrying a flask with a favourite hot drink. If you're not a tea or coffee drinker like me, hot chocolate or hot squash is nice too.

It is often possible to find natural drinking water during your mountain day. The general rule of thumb is if the water is moving (e.g. a fast flowing mountain stream) then it's likely to be OK to drink. You can further protect yourself with purification tablets or water bottles with a built-in filter. In your early mountain climbing days, it's generally better to bring enough water with you for your adventure.

Energy gels

I'm not a huge fan of gels, often used in running or other high-intensity sports. They have a place but it's usually for a short-term hit, and on a long mountain day that's not going to be much use. Plus, consuming more than a couple is likely to make you need to go to the loo. I used to carry a couple in my rucksack to give an emergency boost to clients but I've found that motivation can achieve the same result.

Sunscreen

Believe it or not, the sun does come out and if you're on a big mountain day and walking for several hours, it's important to protect your skin. I've always got a bottle in my rucksack as it's not unusual for the day to start overcast and for the sun to come out in the afternoon. Plus, I have a big forehead that burns in minutes.

Rubbish bag

Don't forget to take everything back off the mountain that you brought with you. In fact, why not go a step further and pick up some litter you find on your way down?

An impressive cloud formation spotted in Eryri (Snowdonia).

9 The Weather

Knowing and understanding the weather on your mountain day is key to making sure you're properly prepared and that you get the most enjoyment out of the experience. For example, having the wrong gear for the conditions could turn a nice day out into a nightmare, or even worse, venturing out in poor visibility or strong winds might lead to serious injury or death.

It's a good idea to check the forecast regularly on the lead up to your day out as it can change a lot in a very short time, particularly in mountainous regions. Aim to look at the weather a few days out, the night before and again in the morning before you set off.

Mountain weather

Beware of using regular weather apps on your smartphone as they'll only be able to tell you what conditions are like at your start point, which can often be at, or close to, sea level. As a very rough guide, temperatures drop around 1°C for every 100m you climb. So, as an example, the village of Llanberis lies at around 100m above sea level and the summit of Yr Wyddfa (Snowdon) is 1,085m, so you could expect it to be at least 10°C cooler at the top (and that's before you take into account wind chill and other factors).

There are two great online resources for mountain weather forecasts in the UK; both of which are easy to use, work well on smartphones and don't cost a penny.

Met Office mountain weather forecasts

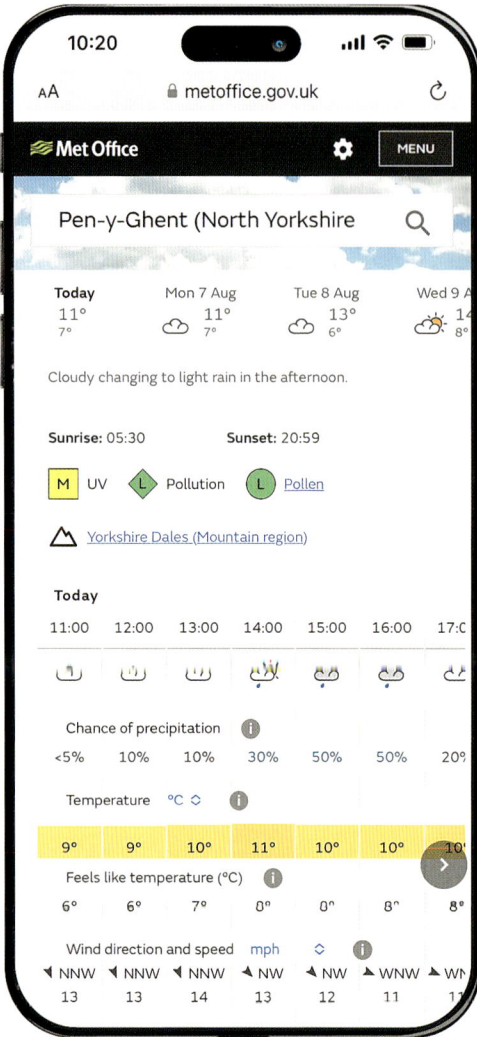

The Met Office website

The UK's Met Office has been predicting the weather for over 150 years and provides twice-daily mountain forecasts for our most popular mountain areas. Designed specifically for walkers, mountaineers and others taking part in outdoor activities, the forecasts are issued daily and cover the next 48 hours, with a brief outlook for the following three days. Updates are issued in the early hours of each morning before 6am. The forecasts are written in plain English but also include detailed meteorological data for those who want it, including wind direction and speed, and temperatures at different altitudes. Particularly useful is the 'feels like temperature', which takes into account additional factors, such as wind chill, to give a more realistic idea of what it will actually feel like at varying points on each mountain. The Met Office also provides seven-day forecasts for specific summits or places of interest within each mountain forecast region. Search online for 'Met Office mountain forecasts'.

Mountain Weather Information Service

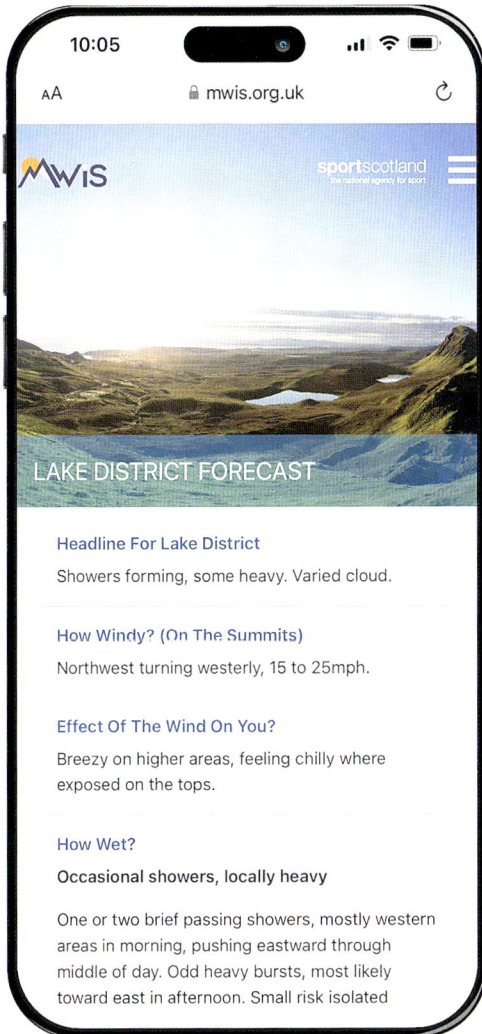

The Mountain Weather Information Service (MWIS) is a dedicated team of professional meteorologists with experience in mountaineering. Set up in 2003 and funded in part by sportscotland with additional sponsorship from other organisations and individuals, the MWIS website receives over seven million hits each year. Their forecasts contain detailed and accessible information, aimed at both novice and experienced mountain users and cover ten upland regions across the country. What I particularly like about MWIS is the simple language they use, with headlines such as 'How Wet?' and 'Chance of Cloud Free Summits' making it easy to understand. You can view a detailed forecast for the next three days and a planning outlook for further ahead. PDFs of their forecasts can often be found pinned up on noticeboards in hostels, cafés and shops as you start your walk and you can access their full forecasts at www.mwis.org.uk, including mobile friendly versions and a low-graphics version for when you might be struggling for Internet signal.

The Mountain Weather Information website

How to deal with changing weather

Having checked the mountain forecast on the morning of your walk and packed your bag accordingly with everything you might need, we should remember that we live in the UK and our weather can change very quickly. This is even more relevant when climbing a mountain.

MOUNTAIN WEATHER INFORMATION SERVICE

www.mwis.org.uk

Yorkshire Dales & North Pennines

The entire Yorkshire Dales National Park and North Pennines AONB, including the Three Peaks and Cross Fell, plus Howgills, also south to Forest of Bowland.

A Day with MWIS - Rheged, Penrith - Thursday 1st June 2023
Full day weather skills course - see our website for info and booking

General Summary for Friday, 5 May, 2023

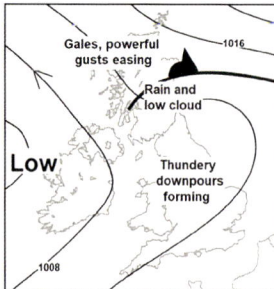

Gales, powerful gusts easing
1016
Rain and low cloud
Low
Thundery downpours forming
1008

British Mountain Summary:

Based on forecast chart for noon 5 May, 2023

Strong southeasterly winds for the Highlands, gale-force with powerful gusts in the morning, tending to ease. Rain and low cloud focused over S-SE Highlands, drier and clearer northwest. Heavy showers and local thunderstorms for England & Wales, clearing later from west.

Headline for Yorkshire Dales & North Pennines

Early rain and low cloud. Showers, local thunderstorms afternoon.

Detailed Forecast for Friday, 5 May, 2023

How windy? (On the summits)	South or southwesterly, speeds varied 10 to 20mph, suddenly very gusty ahead of heavier showers.
Effect of wind on you?	**Mostly fairly small, but occasionally gusty over the tops.**
How wet? (Precipitation and its impact)	**Early rain, heavy showers afternoon, local thunder & lightning.** Rain on and off from before dawn tending to fade out for a time during the morning as a front clears northwards. By afternoon, clusters of heavy showers forming widely, local thunderstorms, later focused toward eastern side of Pennines and perhaps areas toward the south. Fading after sunset.
Cloud on the hills?	**Extensive, lifting with some breaks** Blanket low cloud shrouding the fells in the morning, from low elevations upward western Dales. By afternoon, cloud bases rising, but will drop again around showers. Some breaks toward high tops.
Chance of cloud free summits?	**20% rising to 50%, later 70%**
Sunshine? Air clarity (below cloud)	Extensive cloud, some sun may break through by afternoon into evening. Hazy, murky at times around rain, improving afternoon away from showers.
How Cold? (at 700m)	6C up to 9C out of cloud.
And in the valleys	7C rising to 16C in any sunshine by afternoon, but dropping several degrees in rain.

An example of an MWIS mountain weather forecast.

A beautiful day, but everything below this cloud inversion was shrouded in fog and navigation was challenging.

The two most important things for me, when out walking in less-favourable weather, are to keep warm and stay dry. If you've got the right clothing to enable this, you can get through any sort of weather. Once you start getting cold and wet your decision-making ability deteriorates – which can quickly start causing you problems.

Try and stay ahead of the conditions. As soon as the rain starts coming down, put your waterproofs on. If you start feeling cold while you've stopped for a break, put on another layer. It's easier to stay warm and dry than it is to get warm and dry.

Knowing when to turn back

If you, or someone you're walking with, starts to worry that their clothing or gear isn't up to the conditions, that's when you might want to start thinking about turning back.

As you get more experienced at climbing mountains, you'll get used to what weather is OK for you and what might be 'too much'. Some people hate wind, and I get that it can be scary if you're not used to strong winds in the outdoors. I know what strength of wind will cause me a problem on different mountain days, but there's no point sharing that with you as it's likely my threshold is much higher than yours.

A well-equipped walker, continually monitoring the weather as the day progresses.

Some are quite happy walking in the rain; it doesn't really bother me too much as I have good waterproofs. However, it's definitely less sociable if you've got your hood up and head down, hour after hour.

Something that does keep me off the mountain is lightning. If this is in the forecast and the plan was to lead a group to the summit of a mountain, that's definitely a day for coming up with other options. Being the tallest thing, on top of the highest thing is not the place to be during a lightning storm.

I remember on one occasion having to cancel a day out at the last minute when lightning appeared in the forecast late the evening before. When I woke the next morning, it was raining but didn't seem that bad and I wondered if I'd been overly cautious. A Mountain Rescue friend told me later that day, that a woman had been struck by lightning at the summit and had been helicoptered to hospital. Fortunately, she made a full recovery but I can't imagine it being a pleasant experience.

Knowing how to read a map can lead to more exciting adventures.

10 Navigation

Being able to navigate safely when out in the mountains is an essential skill, and the more time you spend outdoors, the more you will want to develop this skill. I can't teach you how to read a map in this book but I will aim to pass on some useful tips.

Following a route plan in a guidebook or from a smartphone app is OK up to a point, but being able to understand what's around your route, and how to deviate from it should a problem arise, is critical.

What is a map?

In very simple terms, a map is a two-dimensional drawing of something that's three-dimensional. Even if you've never navigated outdoors using an Ordnance Survey map, you're sure to have come across something similar as you wander around a shopping centre looking for the Apple Store, or at a summer festival trying to find the toilets. Most cars are fitted with a satellite navigation system that uses digital mapping such as Google Maps, and even if yours doesn't, you'll have had your head in a road map at some point in your life. All these different types of maps have the same thing in common – they let you visualise a large area on a much smaller sheet of paper or electronic device. The difference in size here is called 'scale' and I'll come on to that a bit later.

Starting the day by looking at route options.

With an outdoors map you can explore a huge network of public footpaths, rights of way and even head completely 'off-piste' in many parts of the country where the Countryside and Rights of Way Act allows (see Chapter 4, Where to Go). You can plan and walk your own routes, learn what's around you while you're out and about, and find where you are if you get lost.

I understand that for many people the sight of a map can fill them with fear, and that you might think it would be easier to crack the Da Vinci Code. However, once you learn what the map represents and get to know a few of the symbols, you'll be amazed at how quickly you can turn it into something useful.

Types of maps

There are a few different types of map suitable for walkers in the British Isles, the most popular of which are produced by the national mapping agency, Ordnance Survey (OS). Formed in the late 1700s, originally for military purposes (as the name suggests), today they provide a huge range of mapping services, predominantly to businesses, with paper maps for walkers only representing a small percentage of its annual revenue. All 243,241 square kilometres of Great Britain have been surveyed by Ordnance Survey's team of cartographers and up to 20,000 changes are put into their database daily.

Ordnance Survey's Explorer range of maps give exceptional detail with a scale of 1:25,000 (1cm on the map representing 25,000cm, or 250m, in real life – more about map scales later on) and many are available as weatherproof versions. They show all public rights of way, footpaths and bridleways and are essential for anyone looking to explore a new area. The downside of Explorer maps is that they can provide too much information, making it tricky to navigate

The familiar look of Ordnance Survey maps.
Photo: Richard Bell on Unsplash.

around 'busy' areas and because these same maps are used by a wide variety of industries, there's information on them that is simply of no use to us as walkers, such as county and parish boundaries which can look annoyingly similar to footpaths.

For slightly less detail but covering a wider area, Ordnance Survey also produces Landranger maps with a scale of 1:50,000. These are more useful for cycling, and activities that might take place over a greater distance. When you progress to winter walking, you'll exclusively use these larger scale maps as you won't be bothered where paths and streams are when they're hidden beneath the snow.

OS maps are universally recognised by walkers and outdoor folk, and they're available everywhere from outdoor shops, online book retailers and from Ordnance Survey

National Navigation Award Scheme

If you're keen to develop your map reading skills, I highly recommend the National Navigation Award Scheme (NNAS). Their Navigator Awards give lovers of the outdoors, whatever their sport, age or fitness, the freedom to explore the paths, trails, hills and mountains of Britain and abroad. Progressing through the Bronze, Silver and Gold Awards will take you from being an absolute map and compass novice right through to be an expert navigator. Search online for 'National Navigation Award Scheme' to find a course near you.

NNAS ™
navigate with confidence

themselves. There's not a patch of land in the UK and Ireland that isn't covered by Ordnance Survey so they're a great place to start.

Newer to the market (although they've been going for over forty years) is Harvey Maps. Unlike Ordnance Survey, whose products are used by many different business sectors, Harvey Maps are designed solely for the outdoor industry, so there's a lot less 'clutter' such as those pesky parish boundaries. They also mostly use 1:25,000 scale maps, but instead of 10m contours (lines printed on the map to indicate height – more about that later) they use 15m contours, meaning there are fewer of them, making the maps easier to read.

Harvey also make 1:40,000 maps with a colour banding system to indicate height, which are generally considered to be more pleasing to the eye than some other maps. All Harvey Maps are printed on tough, waterproof paper and are difficult to damage.

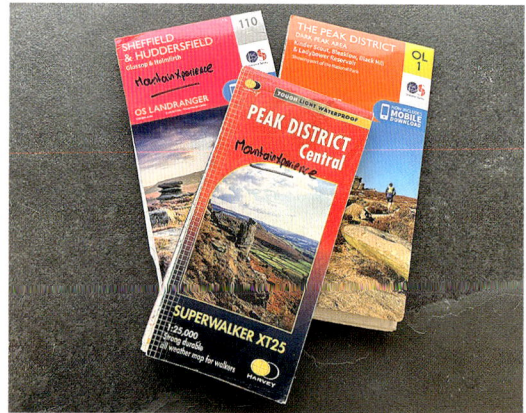

Some of the author's (well thumbed) maps for the Peak District. Each cover approximately the same area but have their individual pros and cons. Try using a variety of maps to find out which works best for you.

You may also come across other types of more bespoke products or maps used for orienteering. They might look different to OS or Harvey maps, but they all do the same thing. Try and get your hands on a few different types so you can experiment a bit to see which you like best.

Digital mapping

As well as traditional paper maps, there are numerous smartphone apps that offer digital mapping, such as the OSMaps app from Ordnance Survey or apps from private companies including AllTrails and Avenza Maps. These have revolutionised the outdoor industry and it's now possible to access digital mapping for the entire UK on your smartphone, wherever you are.

I'm a big fan of the OSMaps app where, for a small annual subscription, you can view any Explorer or Landranger map online or offline, pinpoint your exact location using GPS, and plan your own or follow other people's routes. This is an essential app that everyone walking in the outdoors should download.

However, you should be careful of being solely reliant on digital mapping. It's certainly true that technology is better today than it ever has been, but devices still fail and batteries still run out, so a serious mountain walker venturing into lesser-known territory will always carry a paper map as a backup.

It's also worth being aware of the perils of 'standard' smartphone mapping apps, such as those provided by Google and Apple. Google particularly has done a good job of mapping many footpaths and in 2015 even sent their Street View cameras up Yr Wyddfa (Snowdon), Scafell Pike and Ben Nevis, however, these apps are not designed for walkers and should not be relied on for route finding in the mountains.

The OSMaps app from Ordnance Survey is a valuable tool.

Map scales

The scale of a map is simply the difference in size between what you're looking at on paper (or on screen) and its actual size in real life. For example, Ordnance Survey Explorer maps use a scale of 1:25,000 which means every 1cm on the map represents 25,000cm (or 250m) on the ground. To make this easier to work with we usually talk about 4cm representing 1km and on an OS Explorer map, you'll see this scale clearly marked by the blue grid covering the entire map, where each box is one square kilometre. Grab a ruler and measure any of the blue squares on an OS Explorer map. Each one is exactly 4cm, which means if you walked in a straight line from one blue line to the next, you'd cover exactly 1km.

Different types of maps will have different scales, as they're designed for different purposes. OS Landranger maps use a 1:50,000 scale where 1cm on the map represents 50,000cm (or 500m) on the ground (so 2cm represents 1km at this scale). This is double the scale used on OS Explorer maps and therefore the same size map covers double the area but will, of course, have less detail. Choosing the right map for the right activity is essential. Walkers typically cover smaller areas and prefer to use the detailed mapping provided by a 1:25,000 scale map, whereas cyclists, who can cover a much larger area, are more likely to use a 1:50,000 scale map.

How to read a map

Once you understand what a map represents and get your head around what all the little pictures mean, you'll quickly begin to wonder what all the fuss was about. Every map comes with a key, or legend, which will explain what each line and symbol represents. If you look at the Ordnance Survey Explorer map key you will see it's divided into several distinct groups. **Communications** which cover roads, railways, footpaths, etc; **General Information** which shows how vegetation, boundaries, heights and historical information is displayed and **Tourist and Leisure Information.**

It soon becomes obvious that anything related to tourism is blue, and many of the symbols are pretty easy to work out. The little picture of a tent represents a campsite, a phone receiver is a public telephone, a beer glass for a pub and so on. There's no need to learn all these, as whenever you have a map in your hand, you'll also have the key.

You should also recognise the symbol for roads fairly easily, they'll usually be labelled too (eg A5).

The symbol for a path is a black dashed line, but, just because the path exists it doesn't follow that you have the right to use it. Something you do want to learn pretty quickly are the symbols for the various public rights of way, and how they differ from each other.

A public right of way is just that, something you have the right to move along, although this does depend on how you're doing that, whether by foot, on a bike or horse. Short green dashed lines represent a footpath, which may only be used on foot. Longer green dashed lines are for a bridleway, which can be used on foot, horseback or on bike, although cyclists must give way to horse riders and pedestrians. A line of green plus symbols show a byway open to all traffic; so, as well as people, cyclists and horses you may also encounter cars, motorcycles, etc.

Green diamonds represent a National Trail or long-distance route, and orange short, or long, dashed lines are for a permissive footpath or bridleway, which indicates the landowner has given permission for public use; however, these aren't rights of way and could be withdrawn at any time.

It's important to realise that public rights of way don't always translate to there being something on the ground. They may or may not indicate an actual path (indicated by a

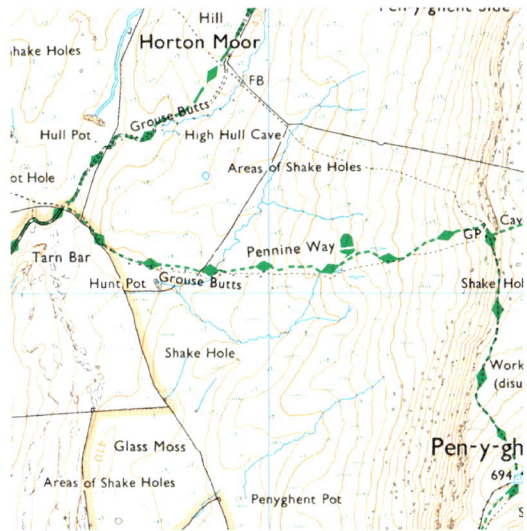

An OS Explorer map showing a section of the Pennine Way National Trail, obvious by its green diamonds.

Map created by Lovell Johns Limited. Based upon Ordnance Survey digital map data © Crown Copyright 2023 Licence Number 43368U. All rights reserved.

black dashed line which can often overlay or run close to the theoretical right of way). Conversely, not all paths are rights of way! Knowing where you can and cannot walk in the countryside is an essential skill.

Interpreting height on a map

Unless you're reading this in the future with a holographic map beaming out of your smartwatch, you're going to need to get to grips with how height is represented on a standard 2D map. Pick up any Ordnance Survey map that covers a mountainous region and you'll see orange or brown lines everywhere. These are contour lines and they join points of equal height. On OS Explorer maps, contour lines are 10m apart, with every fifth line being a bolder, index contour. Look along an index contour line and

When I pick up a map with lots of contour lines, I know I'm going to have tired legs! The map here shows some good examples of how to interpret contours. Around the centre of the map are lots of contour lines close together (indicating steep ground), whereas towards the bottom right, they're spaced much further apart telling us these will be less severe slopes.

Map created by Lovell Johns Limited. Based upon Ordnance Survey digital map data © Crown Copyright 2023 Licence Number 43368U. All rights reserved.

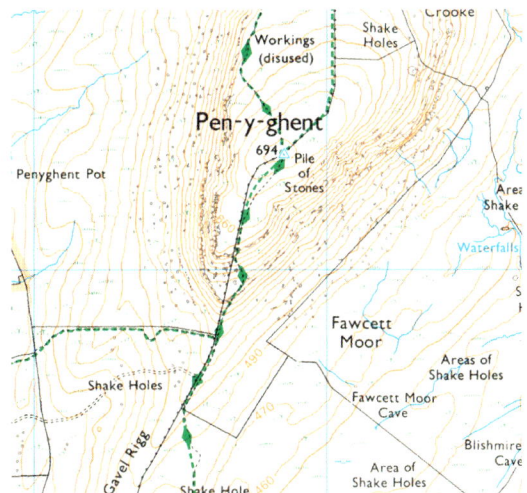

you'll find the actual height, written in metres above sea level. Contour numbers read uphill, so you can also tell where the top and bottom are. It will take you a little while to fully understand contour lines, but the more you use maps the more obvious they will become.

Starting out, all you really need to understand is that the closer contour lines are together, the steeper the gradient. If they're spaced further apart, the gradient is less. Try to relate what contours look like on a map to how the land appears in front of you, to help get a better understanding of how to interpret them.

When you move into more advanced navigation you can use contours to help confirm your location, using skills such as aspect of slope or by simply feeling how the ground changes underfoot.

Understanding grid references

We've established that the maps we use in the outdoors are based on a grid, but how do we use that grid to identify particular features, or give our position? If you look along any of those blue grid lines, you'll see numbers printed on them as well as at the top, bottom and edges of the map. We can identify any particular grid square on the map by taking the horizontal number at the bottom of the grid square and then the vertical number at the left-hand edge of the grid square – put them together and you've got a four-figure grid reference e.g., 8139. Printed in large blue outline type in the corner of Ordnance Survey maps you'll find the national grid reference made up of two letters. This identifies the map sheet you're using, and we add that to the start of our grid reference e.g., SH 8139. It's that easy. Using this method, you can quickly identify any square on a map. (See the route maps in the second half of the book.)

However, we know that each square represents 1km by 1km, and that's quite a large area if you're somewhere in that box on a mountainside waiting for help. It's quite easy to narrow that down even further by imagining a 10x10 grid inside each square, numbered from 0 to 9. The dead centre of a square would be 5,5 and if we add that to our four-figure grid reference, we turn that into a six-figure grid reference e.g., SH 815 395. Now we're able to narrow our search down from 1km^2 to just 100m^2 – a huge improvement.

Grid references are essential for sharing your location with others, such as if an emergency arises and you need assistance from your local Mountain Rescue team.

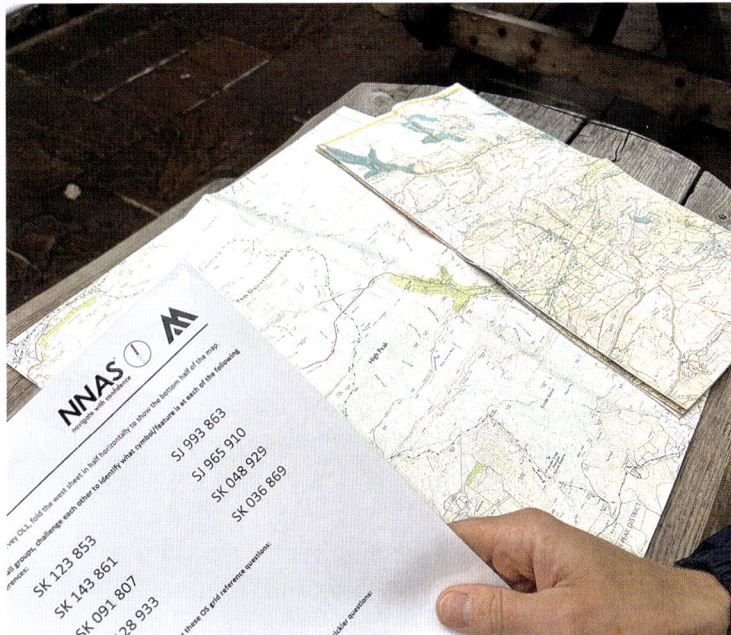

Learning about grid references on a National Navigation Award Scheme course in the Peak District.

OS Locate

Ordnance Survey provides a free smartphone app called OS Locate, which will instantly give you your six-figure grid reference for wherever you are. It doesn't need an Internet connection and is simple to use. Go and download it now from your device's app store.

Ordnance Survey's free OS Locate app is the fast and easy way to get the six-figure grid reference for your current location

Orientating a map

Knowing how to hold or 'orientate' your map is an essential skill that you should learn right from the off. We already know that a map is a two-dimensional drawing of our three-dimensional world, so when we're standing in the outdoors with our map in our hand, it makes sense that we hold it in a way that represents what we see in front of us. This is 'orientating the map', and we do this using linear features such as paths, tracks, roads or boundaries like walls or fences as 'handrails'. Look up at the landscape in front of you and look for something obvious; such as a road, find that road on your map then, holding the map still in front of you, move your body around until the general direction of the road matches the markings on the map. Once you've done this, the map should accurately represent what you're seeing in front of you. As you get more experienced, you can stay facing your direction of travel and instead, turn the map.

Get into the habit of re-orientating your map every time you pick it up, as having a correctly orientated map makes navigating much easier.

Another technique for orientating a map is to place a compass anywhere on the map and rotate your body until the red needle is pointing to the top of your map. It doesn't matter which way the compass is pointing, just the needle. This is quick and easy, however, as a beginner you probably won't be using a compass a great deal, and it also takes away some of the skill of learning how to orientate a map from the landscape alone.

Holding your map correctly is something else you should get good at quickly. Nothing screams 'newbie' more than someone struggling with a fully unfolded OS map flapping in the wind. On any particular day, you're rarely going to need more than a 'folded' section, so get used to preparing your map before you start. Bend it, shape it, fold it any way you need to, so that the bit of the map you're working with that day is quickly accessible. I was also taught to tear off the cover and leave it at home as it serves little purpose. It does make the map easier to fold but I'm not sure there's a huge weight saving benefit there.

Some people like to hang their map around their neck in a map case. I like that your map is protected that way and it's easily accessible, but I don't like having something hanging around your neck all day, plus it definitely doesn't look cool! You'll often find that walking trousers and outdoor jackets have larger-than-normal pockets designed specially to accommodate maps.

Learning how to walk with a map is really useful. I hate seeing people walking with their heads constantly in the map, ignoring the beautiful scenery around them. Look at

Holding your map so it accurately reflects what you can see in front of you is called 'orientating the map'.

the map, get the information you need, then put it away. We use control, collecting and catching features to make mental notes about what we expect to see as we're walking; I'll explain more about them in the next section.

Runners and orienteers will often 'thumb' the map - this is the process of keeping your thumb on the map to remind you where you are. This is because they're moving quickly and constantly referring back to it. This can be useful for walkers … but you tend not to need to be going back to the map quite so frequently.

Walking with a map

I've already mentioned the perils of walking with your head in the map. Apart from the fact that you're missing everything that's going on around you and that it can make you rather dull company, you also run the risk of tripping. To get around this, we make mental notes about short sections of our route with a few collecting and catching features to check we're on the right path (oooh a pun!).

For example, we're going to walk a short stretch of path from A to B (they're our control points – the start and finish of our current leg). On the map we're looking for some points along the route that will help reinforce that we're going the right way.

It's best to fold your map before you start walking!

For example, we're going to cross a footbridge, pass a wall on our left, the path then bends sharply to the right, etc. These are our collecting features, sometimes called tick features, as we're going to mentally tick them off as we walk. We might also note that when the path bends sharply to the right, if we were to mistakenly carry straight on, we'd come to a wall. This is a catching feature which is something to tell us we've gone wrong.

Once we've made this mental note of our control points, collecting and catching features, we can put the map away and enjoy our walk, mentally ticking them off as we progress. We then only need to refer back to the map if we come across something we weren't expecting or hit a catching feature, or when we get to our next control point.

Some definitions

Control – the start and finish points of our current leg.

Collecting features / tick off features – things we're looking for along our leg to confirm we're going the right way.

Catching features – something that if we reach, we know we've gone the wrong way.

Measuring distance on a map

It can be useful to know how far you're going to travel and how long it is likely to take you. You can use your map to measure distance and then some simple maths can give you an idea of time.

We know that a 1:25,000 Ordnance Survey map is covered by a blue grid made up of 4cm squares and that those 4cm squares represent 1,000m or 1km. So, if we're walking along a path that's (pretty much) horizontal (east / west) or vertical (north / south) then we can use those grid lines to give us an estimate of distance. Of course, most paths don't run horizontal or vertical or even in a straight line, so we need another method.

To measure distance between two points that aren't dead straight you can use a piece of string. If you carry a compass, then the loop string is perfect. Place the start of the string (or mark your compass string with a permanent marker and start from there) at point A, and then manipulate the string along your route until you get to point B. When you've got the length of string for the distance you want to measure, use the blue grid lines on the map to give you a pretty good idea of the distance; for example, if the string covers two and a half squares, your distance will be 2.5km.

For an even more accurate measurement, take your string to the scale bar at the bottom of Ordnance Survey maps or in the legend on Harvey Maps. It looks a bit like a ruler and you'll be able to measure exact distances.

Two quick and easy ways to measure distance on a map. The first with a handy measuring card, the second using the romer on the edge of a compass. With both options, be sure to use the correct scale.

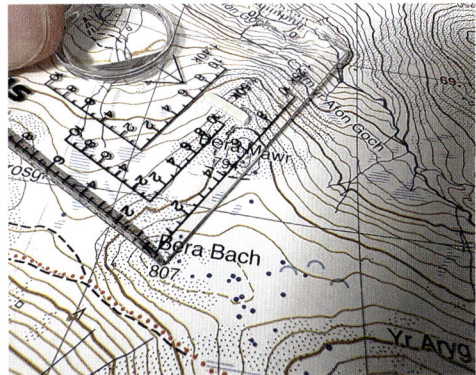

HARVEY

© HARVEY Maps

If you're carrying a compass, you'll usually see a ruler along the edge which you can also use to measure distance. Just like with the string, place the edge of the compass starting at 0cm on your start point and then weave it along your route. Take the measurement and convert it to metres, remembering the scale you're using. For example, 6cm on a 1:25,000 map will be 1,500m or 1.5km, but 6cm on a 1:50,000 map would be 3,000m or 3km.

To get around the problem of trying to do maths on the side of a mountain, a good compass will also have a romer along one or two edges. This is a marked-out 'ruler' often for a few different scales. So, if you're walking with a 1:25,000 map, place the 1:25k romer on the map along your route and you'll get an accurate distance measurer without having to do any conversions.

You can also get a transparent romer made of plastic that you can lay over your map and do much the same thing.

Measuring distance on the ground

If we know a particular leg we need to walk is a certain distance, being able to know when we've covered that distance is really useful. One way we do this is by counting steps or to use the navigation term 'pacing'. On flat, level ground humans naturally walk at a set pace, and once you've worked out your pace count, you can then use that to know how far you're walked. We normally measure pace count over 100m, so you need to accurately measure 100m then simply walk it, counting every other step. Do it a few times to get the average, although it should always be pretty similar.

Now you know your own pace count, you know that when you've walked that number of paces across flat, level ground you've covered 100m. Double it and you've covered 200m. Get used to pacing in 100m legs as trying to count beyond that is quite difficult If you need to walk 500m pick up five stones and drop one each time you count to a hundred then start again. Some people put beads or toggles on their compass string or rucksack strap for this purpose.

Pacing is particularly useful in poor visibility where it might not be easy to see objects in the distance. The downside of pacing is that the concentration required in counting kind of makes you dull company. In good visibility it is more usual to estimate distance covered by the time it should take.

Turning distance into time

Knowing how far you're going to walk is handy, but knowing how long it should take you is even more useful. We can calculate this pretty accurately using a couple of different methods.

Assuming we're walking on a relatively flat, level surface, most people walk at a steady pace of between 3kph and 5kph, with the lower end being a gentle stroll and upper end a brisk pace. Of course, families with young children might walk slower than 3kph and particularly fit folk might be closer to 6kph. The more time you spend outdoors, the better you'll get at judging your own walking speed. Knowing this, we can do some simple maths to calculate how long it will take us to walk a certain distance. Taking the average walking speed of 4kph, it would take an hour to walk 4km, or 15 minutes to walk 1km, 7.5 minutes to walk 500m or 1.5 minutes to cover 100m. So, if our next leg is 300m, we should expect to cover that ground in four and a half minutes. You'll be surprised how accurate this method is.

We can put this data into a timing chart like this:

Distance (m)	3kph	4kph	5kph
1000	20 min	15 min	12 min
900	18 min	13.5 min	11 min*
800	16 min	12 min	10 min*
700	14 min	10.5 min	8.5 min*
600	12 min	9 min	7 min*
500	10 min	7.5 min	6 min
400	8 min	6 min	5 min*
300	6 min	4.5 min	3.5 min*
200	4 min	3 min	2.5 min*
100	2 min	1.5 min	1 min*

I've rounded off many of the 5kph timings to make them easier to work with. This is indicated by an asterisk.

Creating your own timing chart is really simple (you're welcome to print the one above and laminate it), but I'm a big fan of the Navigators Timing Card available from ShavenRaspberry. They're printed on credit card sized tough plastic and are a great addition to any outdoor kit. Search for ShavenRaspberry Navigators Timing Card online.

ShavenRaspberry Navigators Timing Card

There are of course a few anomalies to this method. What if the ground isn't flat and level? What if there's snow? What if we're walking uphill? Or carrying a really heavy rucksack? Luckily, we have an answer for that too. Back in Victorian times, Scottish mountaineer William Naismith came up with a rule for calculating the time required to walk a set distance while factoring in height. Very simply, going uphill – add one minute for each 10m contour line you cross, up to a maximum of three contours in 100m distance, and coming downhill subtract 20 seconds for each 10m contour crossed, up to the same maximum. It's also worth noting that any more than 30m of vertical ascent in any 100m would make the ground too steep to use this method, but it's unlikely you'll be walking on that sort of terrain at your current ability level.

According to ShavenRaspberry's Navigators Timing card, if you're walking in the dark you would halve your daytime walking speed, if you're carrying a heavy rucksack or walking into a strong headwind, you would subtract 1kph.

This is, however, starting to get into more advanced navigation territory, so just remember that if you're walking uphill you're going to be moving slower, and when you're coming down again you'll be a bit quicker.

Climbing mountains can be a great family activity.   Photo: Sandra Foyt, Dreamstime.com

11 Walking with Children

Children love being outdoors, and the added achievement of reaching the top of a mountain should make for an even more enjoyable day out for the family – but knowing how to keep them entertained is essential for group harmony, and for ensuring that they'll want to do it again. The key is getting them started when they're young. I've met a five-year-old and his Mum at the top of a mountain, and you'll often see babies and toddlers smiling in back carriers (usually with tired parents smiling a little less!).

I'm constantly amazed at how far young children will walk in the mountains. With the right adult support, they can tackle the biggest mountain days alongside you.

The more kids walk locally, the easier they'll find it when it comes to climbing a mountain. It's not always about how physically fit they are – it's as much about their mental attitude and that can often be the biggest challenge for parents. In the same way when children say they're hungry, it usually means they're bored; when they say they're tired it can often mean the same thing. It's amazing how much further they can go when they have an activity or task to occupy them, or a game to get them smiling.

When I'm guiding with families, I love getting kids involved with route finding. For younger children, I'll tell them what I'm expecting to see coming up (such as a path junction, a gate or a big rock) and that I need their help to spot it. For teenagers, I might give them a map or use digital mapping and get them to lead a leg.

Many children today have a Fitbit activity tracker, smartwatch or a similar step-counter and if you're out on a really adventurous day, it's very likely to be their highest ever step count. This can act as a fantastic motivational tool.

My nephew at seven years old was thrilled when he reached 32,000 steps at the end of a day of fairly easy walking in the Peak District.

All of the routes in the back of this book are suitable for children after a bit of practise, some prep work and these useful tips.

Be realistic

While children have a lot of energy and ambition, if the furthest you've ever walked as a family is to and from your local park, then heading straight for Ben Nevis is probably going to be a bit much. Get them used to walking longer distances and explore more achievable hills closer to home first – certainly for younger kids of infant school age. That's not to say bigger hills and mountains are out of the question. If you have a fit and healthy child in junior school who's used to exercise, then go for it.

Make sure they're kitted out properly

You'll be well used to making the kids put on their coats before heading to the park but making sure they have the right outdoor gear is as important for them, if not more, than it is for you.

Let them have their own (mini) rucksack, and pack their own waterproofs and snacks, etc (being sure to not make it too heavy or you'll be carrying it later!).

Get the kids involved with route planning. Giving them their own map can help keep them on task.

Kids are smaller (babies even smaller still) and with a much bigger surface area will lose heat considerably faster than adults. Look out for early signs that they might be getting cold or wet and take action ASAP.

Climbing a mountain with a baby or a toddler in a back carrier is a lovely idea but can be potentially dangerous for the child, particularly when they're immobile. If you are keen to do this, make sure they're wrapped up well and stop and check on them regularly.

Be aware that you're going to be in a remote location, and if something goes wrong you will be much further away from help than if you're at home. Something to think about.

Get them involved

The easiest way to keep their minds occupied is to keep them busy. Discuss the day's plans in advance of the walk, show them where they'll be going on a map, talk to them about how excited they're going to feel standing on the top of a mountain and what an achievement it will be. Let them pick their favourite snacks (climbing a mountain is a great excuse to combine their normal healthy foods with some high fat and sugary treats for extra energy).

If you're using a map, let them have their own copy. A common navigation technique is to use 'collecting features' to make sure you're on the right track. (Learn more in Chapter 10, Navigation). Rather than walking with your head in the map, you'll take note of a few features ahead that you should pass as you're walking and then tick them off as you reach each point. For example, crossing a stile, the path bending sharply to the left, a fence coming in from the right. Giving children these features to look out for is a great way to keep them involved, and if they're old enough they can even identify the features on the map themselves.

My niece and nephew were six and seven when I gave them their first Ordnance Survey map and took them on a walk in the Peak District. They loved learning about route choice and what the different map symbols meant. Since then, they've gone on to earn their Bronze Navigator Award with the National Navigation Award Scheme.

The National Navigation Award Scheme is suitable for all ages.

Be positive

Granted, this is great advice for dealing with children in any situation; but when you're halfway up mountain and listening to complaints of being 'exhausted' and "I'm bored"; the more positive you are, the more that will rub off on them.

In the late nineties I wrote a dissertation on assertive discipline, which is all about praising good behaviour and ignoring (some) bad behaviour. It's amazing how well this works, and dealing with tired children in this situation is just the same. Telling them to 'stop whinging' or 'hurry up' is unlikely to produce any useful results, whereas 'you're doing brilliantly' and 'we're nearly there' will give them the motivation they need (assuming you are nearly there).

Remember, however tired you might be, you need to convey confidence to your children to keep them going. Happy children make happy parents!

Bribe them!

OK, this probably doesn't feature in many parenting books, but big mountain days sometimes call for big bribes! Maybe we shouldn't talk about 'bribing' children – let's call it 'motivational encouragement'. Anything from supplying sweets along the way, to the promise of an ice cream when they get down. I remember working with one lovely family who rocked up in the morning with a Tesco carrier bag full of snacks. Let's just say it didn't stay full for very long!

Play games

I've come up with some ridiculous games on the spot, when I've felt I might be losing kids' attention. Depending on their age and your location you can make up any sort of fun activity to keep them on task. Something as simple as spotting the next person wearing a yellow jacket, or guessing what colour trousers the next person to appear out of the mist will be wearing, seeing how many people you can get to wave as they walk past, counting 100 steps in your head and, the all-time classic, who can count the highest number of steps without talking (you usually only get to play this once!).

Here's a couple of my favourites that work well on the mountain:

Scavenger Hunt

This can be prepared in advance or you can 'wing it' on the day. Simply give the kids a written or verbal list of things to collect / look out for on their walk, such as:
- Something green
- A piece of litter (pick it up and take it home with you!)
- Someone wearing a brightly coloured coat
- A stone or rock bigger than their fist
- A signpost
- Someone younger than them

The list is endless …

The Alphabet Game

One of my favourites. Take it in turns to 'spot' something beginning with each letter of the alphabet, starting with 'A' (you might need to pass on Q and Z).

You can also play this with categories such as countries, animals, boys / girls names, etc.

Myths and legends

Kids love stories, and mountains are full of them. Do a bit of online research before your mountain day and find out some of the local myths and legends relating to your mountain.

Many mountain names are shrouded in mythology and folklore. Take Snowdon's Welsh name Yr Wyddfa which, legend has it, is the final resting place of Rhita Gawr, a fearsome giant. He challenged King Arthur to combat but was defeated. According to legend, the cairn on the summit of Yr Wyddfa marks the final resting place of Rhita Gawr. Yr Wyddfa roughly translates to 'tomb' or 'cairn'.

(There aren't many cheery legends!)

Develop their future

If your kids show an interest in the outdoors and would like to develop their skills further, encourage them to join a local youth group such as the Scout or Guide Associations. As they get a bit older, find out if their school or college is involved with The Duke of Edinburgh's Award (DofE). This is a fantastic way to develop a young person's love of the outdoors through a wide range of activities.

If mountain skills or map reading excites them, then sign them up for an outdoor course. Find out more in Chapter 17, Where Can I Learn More?

Be certain your pooch is up for the long day out!   Photo: Yelizaveta Tomashevska, Dreamstime.com

12 Walking with Dogs

Dogs are a common sight in the mountains and, if you have one, you'll probably want to share your mountain day with yours but remember, that as well as being a physical challenge for you, it may be a much greater challenge for your pet. You should be sure your dog is up for the job if you want to avoid having to carry it down.

Much of the countryside is farmland and you'll often see sheep grazing at all times of the year, so it's vital that you keep dogs under close control. Don't assume that just because you can't see any sheep that it's safe for your dog to be off the lead – you also need to consider ground nesting birds which you may not be able to see.

If you're not 100% confident about how your dog behaves around livestock, you must keep it on a lead at all times. Sheep worrying is a real problem for farmers. It's a dog's natural instinct to chase but even if a dog doesn't actually catch a sheep, the stress of being chased can cause sheep to die or pregnant ewes to miscarry. Sheep fleeing from dogs are often killed or injured in the process. Sheep aren't the brightest of animals and when subject to stress, it's been known that they can run right off the edge of a mountain to their death.

Dogs are very welcome in the mountains but will probably need to stay on a lead throughout the day.

Sheep worrying is a criminal offence, and farmers are legally entitled to shoot dogs that are endangering their sheep. This is a situation that nobody wants and is easily avoided by keeping your dog under close control.

The advice below is taken from The Countryside Code and sums up nicely how you should behave with dogs. You can also find more information on the Dog Walking Code from Natural Resources Wales.

A sign spotted in the Peak District reminding dog owners of the real threat that exists.

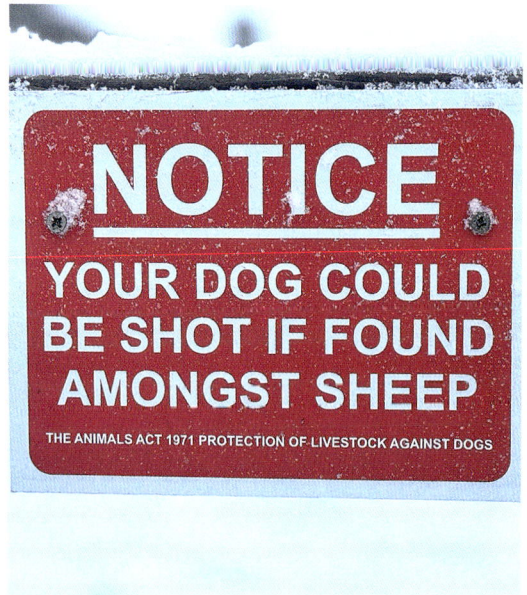

NOTICE

YOUR DOG COULD BE SHOT IF FOUND AMONGST SHEEP

THE ANIMALS ACT 1971 PROTECTION OF LIVESTOCK AGAINST DOGS

Extract from The Countryside Code

Always keep dogs under control and in sight.

The countryside, parks and the coast are great places to exercise your dog but you need to consider other users and wildlife.

Keep your dog under effective control to make sure it stays away from wildlife, livestock, horses and other people unless invited. You should:

- Always keep your dog on a lead or in sight.

- Be confident your dog will return on command.

- Make sure your dog does not stray from the path or area where you have right of access.

Always check local signs as there are situations when you must keep your dog on a lead for all or part of the year. Local areas may also ban dogs completely, except for assistance dogs. Signs will tell you about these local restrictions.

It is good practice, wherever you are, to keep your dog on a lead around livestock.

On Open Access land and at the coast, you must put your dog on a lead around livestock. Between 1 March and 31 July, you must have your dog on a lead on Open Access land, even if there is no livestock on the land. These are legal requirements.

A farmer can shoot a dog that is attacking or chasing livestock. They may not be liable to compensate the dog's owner.

Let your dog off the lead if you feel threatened by livestock or horses. Do not risk getting hurt protecting your dog. Releasing your dog will make it easier for you both to reach safety.

Dog poo – bag it and bin it – any public waste bin will do.

Always clean up your dog's poo because it can cause illness in people, livestock and wildlife.

Never leave bags of dog poo around, even if you intend to pick them up later. Deodorised bags and containers can make bags of dog poo easier to carry. If you cannot find a public waste bin, you should take it home and use your own bin.

Keep your dog under effective control to make sure it stays away from wildlife, livestock, horses and other people, unless invited.

Climbing mountains solo is a brilliant way to 'detox' – but there are a few important things you should know.

13 Going it Alone

More and more people are venturing out into the mountains on their own, and it's no wonder when you consider the amount of space and the abundance of peaceful solitude available. When I'm not leading groups or walking with friends, I love being alone outdoors. It's perfectly possible to go a whole day without bumping into anyone. It gives me time to think, come up with new ideas and plan future projects, or I can just switch off and enjoy the silence. There are a few considerations to take into account however, as there are obviously greater risks when exploring remote areas alone.

Never be afraid of walking on your own. Just take a few extra precautions to ensure your safety.

Tell someone what you're doing

Be sure to let a loved one or friend know that you're going for a walk on your own, and give them some information that might be useful if anything were to go wrong.

I'd suggest letting them know where you're planning to go, where you're going to start from and a rough idea of what time you'll be back. If you're following a set route, for example from the back of this book or from another source, or if you've prepared a route

Stop and say hello to people you pass along the way. You're not on the London Underground now!

card yourself, then leaving a copy of that behind is also really useful. And of course, let your contact know when you're back home, safe.

Talk to people

I'm well known as something of a 'talker', particularly when out on the hills. Nobody is exempt from a 'good morning / bore da' or 'how's your day going?' as you pass each other, and more so when I'm walking alone and come across other lone walkers. You can usually tell whether someone is quite happy with a head nod or who's up for a bit of a chat. People walking in the countryside are usually friendly folk, and it's always amusing how chatty people can be with each other compared to how they might behave walking along a street in their home town. As a professional mountaineer, I also use this opportunity to offer any help if someone sounds like they might need it. If you're on your way down a hill, passing others on their way up, people always want to know if they're 'nearly there yet' and giving them a bit of motivation can make all the difference. I also find it useful to ask those who might have already been to a summit about the conditions there. What they tell you can be really useful.

Invest in some safety tech

When you move on from being a 'beginner' and find yourself walking alone more often, particularly in exposed and remote regions, you may want to consider investing in a personal locator beacon (PLB). Traditionally used by those at sea, they've been licensed to use inland since 2012, and even though in the UK the system is managed by the Maritime & Coastguard Agency (MCA), as the devices typically broadcast your GPS location, they will be able to tell that you're up a mountain and not at sea and liaise with mountain rescue services to get help to you. PLBs don't rely on mobile phone networks and so are particularly useful in remote parts of the country.

When activated, along with your location they also transmit a unique code which can be matched with information held in the UK Distress & Security Beacon Registry. The emergency services will use this information to attempt to contact you and your next of kin to ascertain more about the situation and to ensure the activation is genuine, so it's essential that when you buy a new one or move house, you update your details with the MCA.

The devices are small, rugged and lightweight. There are no monthly subscriptions and the battery life should last upwards of six years (although mine is nine years old and still shows a full battery). I have an older version of the FastFind 220 from McMurdo which, at the time of writing, costs around £200. At this price it's definitely an investment and really only for those who are perhaps exploring 'off grid' more than a weekend hiker.

The main downside of PLBs is that the communication is only one-way, so you're only going to want to use them in the most serious emergency and when you can't get hold of mountain rescue using a mobile phone.

More modern (and expensive) devices are also available but are typically aimed at those leading groups or travelling internationally. A popular example is the Garmin inReach® Mini satellite communicator which, from anywhere on the planet, will allow you to maintain off-the-grid contact. It's pocket-sized, durable and impact resistant and water-rated. Using

The author's aging McMurdo FastFind 210 Personal Locator Beacon.

the satellite network means you stay connected even where mobile phones fail; with location sharing, two-way messaging, social media capabilities and contact with other inReach's all possible in no service areas. You can also send interactive SOS alerts, and it will also put you through to Garmin's International Emergency Response Coordination Centre (IERCC), a 24 / 7 staffed emergency response centre. However, you will have to fork out several hundred pounds for one of these and pay a monthly subscription to Garmin, so it's not something most will use in the UK.

The Garmin inReach® Mini 2 is most likely to appeal to those travelling internationally.   Photo: REMEC

Remember your mobile phone

An absolute necessity in this day and age. Make sure you have your mobile phone with you, make sure it's fully charged before you start your day and make sure it's somewhere dry and secure. Ideally carry a battery bank with you too (see Chapter 8, What to Take with You).

Some of the latest mobile phone tech also offers emergency SOS via satellite, to text the emergency services when you're outside mobile and Wi-Fi coverage. I can see this technology becoming quite standard in the near future.

Composting toilets are commonplace in other countries, but would they cope with the footfall on some of our popular mountain paths?
Photo: Peter Wollinga, Dreamstime.com

14 Going to the Toilet

Why are you laughing? It's something we all do every day, and usually with very little thought. However, when you're out in the countryside or halfway up a mountain and potentially several hours away from a proper toilet, it suddenly becomes more of an issue. Perhaps a bigger concern for women than it might be for men, who will typically go anywhere without a care, there are some rules and useful tips I'd like to share.

Firstly, the worst thing you can do is avoid going to the toilet by not drinking. Taking on liquids during your mountain day is essential. OK, you might be able to get away with it on a shorter walk but inevitably you're going to be walking uphill, sweating away fluids and burning energy, so it's vital that you stay hydrated.

Anyone with young kids knows that you don't leave the house without making them go to the toilet and it's no different for you. Many of the mountain walks in the back of this book start from car parks with public toilets. They may not always be the best (you're likely to have to fight off a spider or two) but they're better than nothing, so be sure you go before you start your adventure.

However, there's really no avoiding it; you're going to need a wee at some point during your day in the mountains so it's important to find the right place to go. For gentlemen it might just be walking a reasonable distance off the path, waiting for others to walk out of sight and then let rip. Always get as far off the path as possible. Nobody wants to see a pool of wee as they're walking up the mountain. Avoid places where people might stop for a rest for the same reason. This is even more important on popular walking routes. Imagine the smell if hundreds of people did their business in the same spot every day. Never wee in, or close to, running water as you don't know who might be drinking that water further downstream.

For ladies, you're probably going to want a bit more privacy. This can be easier said than done, particularly on popular routes on busy summer weekends. Head away from the path everyone is walking along and aim for that big rock. I guess the best advice I can give is to be quick! You must take any used toilet paper or tissues home with you, preferably in a bag. On an overnight expedition you might dig a hole and burn the paper, but this isn't really practical on a day out and nobody wants to see toilet paper or human faeces littering the countryside.

If you're walking as part of a group, don't be shy. You don't need to explicitly say what you're going to do. I usually just say something along the lines of "I'll catch you up" – people understand what's happening.

Number two's are a bit trickier. I would imagine that most of us can go out for a day's walk without needing to worry too much about this, but an upset tummy or that big curry the night before can play havoc with your insides. (If you're ever lucky enough to meet me in person, ask me about my emergency toilet dash while trekking in Nepal. It's definitely not a story for putting in print!)

There really is no satisfactory solution here. Again, on multi-day trips, you'll carry a small plastic spade so you can dig a hole, do your stuff and bury it (after burning any toilet roll/tissues) but this isn't something I'd suggest you need to carry with you routinely.

The same principles apply though. If you really have to go, move well off the path you're walking on, find something for privacy, use whatever you can to dig the best hole possible, do your business then cover it up. If you've used toilet paper or tissues you must burn and bury it or, even better, take it away with you. Never simply leave it behind.

Don't neglect your personal hygiene either, so remember to clean your hands using antibacterial hand sanitiser.

Nobody wants to see used toilet paper (and worse) littering the mountains.

It's unlikely in your early mountain climbing days that you'll find yourself needing to go while walking in winter, but this became a big problem in the Scottish Cairngorms where people thought they were burying human waste in the snow, only for it to 'magically' reappear in the spring. As a result, the brilliantly named 'Cairngorm Poo Project' was introduced, where mountaineers would take poo bags and special containers out with them, for them to bring back at the end of their adventure and dispose of the waste safely, back at the car park. As yucky as this might seem, it's a brilliant idea.

Periods

Dealing with your period whilst in the mountains is a very normal part of life outdoors and shouldn't be embarrassing. Much of the advice above also applies to managing your period, but you'll probably need to bring some extra things with you if it coincides with your mountain climb.

If possible, plan around your period so that you're doing less on your heavier days. Stay hydrated and well-nourished, and keep some period bits such as spare sanitary items and painkillers in your personal first aid kit. Pack a waterproof nappy bag or container / bag to deal with used products and ensure you take all your rubbish away with you.

Dark coloured poo or nappy bags can be useful for disposal.

When you've found some privacy, take time to prepare all your items, clean your hands using hand sanitiser and lay out a nappy or poo bag beside you. Change your sanitary items and wrap your used items in toilet roll / tissue, before double bagging them in poo / nappy bags, and then storing them in a side pocket of your rucksack or in a dedicated tub inside.

If you use a menstrual cup, take time to prepare your items and clean your hands. Create a hole in the ground and pour the contents in and/or wash away with water if possible. Clean out your cup with preboiled water or use tissue, then re-insert and clean your hands again.

Advice for women

Harriet MacMillan is a mountaineer based in the Lake District and has written about the difficulties women face in the outdoors. Find out more about how she can help at *www.navigationwithharriet.co.uk.*

Volunteer wardens picking up litter in the mountains.   *Photo: Tony Ellis*

15 Litter

You might think it sad that there's a chapter in this book about litter in the mountains, and you'd be absolutely right. I'm sad that I'm even writing this. But it happens, and while some of it is down to a minority of people not caring about our environment, other litter is a bit more complicated.

It shouldn't come as a shock that you're expected to take everything away with you. You've seen what the Countryside Code (see Chapter 6) has to say on the matter. If you've brought food up the mountain, then you should be able to take the wrappers home. If you have single-use plastic bottles, make sure they go back in your bag. Assuming you've eaten what you've brought, it should be lighter on the way down. In fact, why not go a step further and pick up some litter you see during your day. If every walker collected just one piece of rubbish, the mountains would be completely litter free. I often carry a rubbish bag with me when I'm out walking for this precise reason.

Working in the mountains, I sometimes hear walkers complaining about the lack of bins. When I politely question them about who might be responsible for emptying these bins (are the local council expected to run a little bin lorry up and down the mountain each night?) they quickly realise their error. It should be the norm that we take all our litter away with us.

Litter left in the doorway of the Hafod Eryri visitor centre at the summit of Yr Wyddfa (Snowdon).   *Photo: Tony Ellis*

The best option is to take litter home with you and recycle / dispose of it at home. Bins in remote mountain car parks might not get emptied that frequently and there's an added risk that animals will get at the waste.

In North Wales, plans are afoot to make Yr Wyddfa (Snowdon) the first plastic free mountain. Try to avoid bringing single-use plastic bottles and instead buy a reusable water bottle or flask.

There is a common misconception about fruit waste such as banana skins and orange peels. When I volunteer with my local mountain warden team, a large amount of what we collect is fruit waste. But hang on, peels and skins are biodegradable, aren't they? Well, yes, and no. They might degrade relatively quickly in areas where they're grown, but we don't grow many bananas or oranges in the UK so they'll hang around for quite a while. Think also about the numbers. Some popular mountains have tens or hundreds of thousands of visitors each year. If everyone left their banana skins beside the path it would look horrific. So please, carry your fruit waste with you off the mountain.

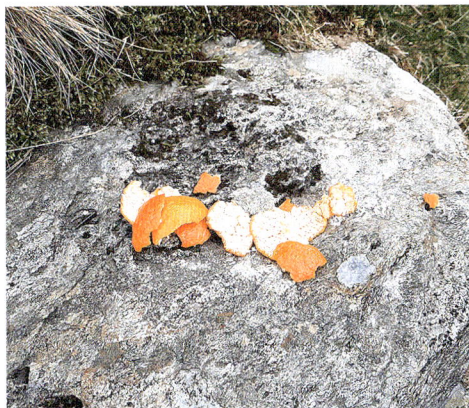

Fruit waste found on typical mountain day.   *Photos: Tony Ellis*

How long does it take?

If you'd like to learn more about how long it takes different waste material to degrade in the mountains, use your favourite online search engine to search for 'Mike Raine biodegradable experiment'.

Mike is a hugely experienced mountaineering instructor with a passion for the environment. His experiment to see how long it takes popular mountain waste to degrade will shock you.

Volunteers

The UK's mountains are well looked after by teams of volunteers who patrol popular mountain paths each week, chatting to walkers and picking up litter. In Eryri (Snowdonia), the 40-strong volunteer warden team are out every weekend, bank holiday and often in the week too, working alongside members of other organisations such as Caru Eryri. In the Lakes, The National Trust and Friends of the Lake District regularly organise litter picks and the John Muir Trust, Nevis Landscape Partnership and Friends of Nevis keep Ben Nevis litter free.

Other organisations such as Trash Free Trails, The Real Three Peaks Challenge and the British Mountaineering Council are also heavily involved in keeping our mountains litter free.

Without these people giving up of their time freely, our mountains would be a much worse place. If you think you could offer time to help keep the countryside litter free, why not contact one of the organisations above to see how you can get involved. And remember to stop and say 'thank you' if you see litter pickers out and about.

Volunteer wardens on Yr Wyddfa (Snowdon) picking up litter at the summit.

Llanberis Mountain Rescue Team working alongside HM Coastguard, Yr Wyddfa.   Photo: Rich Griffiths

16 What to do if Something Goes Wrong

If you're well prepared, have planned your day right and followed all the excellent advice in this book then, just like the vast majority of mountain days, yours should go without a hiccup. However, knowing what to do if something does go wrong is essential, as you never know what you might come across on a day out.

Being prepared is the key to avoiding problems on the mountain. That covers everything from making sure you know your route plan, have shared it with a friend or family member, that you're wearing the right clothes and have the right equipment (and know how to use it), that you've checked the weather forecast and understand what it's going to do that day, that you know where you're going to park, what time you estimate you'll be back, and so on. The more preparation you put into your day out, the less likelihood of something going wrong, and like most things, the more you do it, the easier it becomes. I can pull together what I need for a day out in just a few minutes now, whereas in my early days I would obsess the night before about exactly what was in my rucksack.

But no matter how well you prepare and how ready you are for your adventure, there's still a possibility that something might go wrong – either for yourself, a member of your party or another walker you come across.

The key to managing any mountain incident is to remain calm.

Forgetting something

It is truly a horrible feeling when you get out of your car after a long, early morning drive, look up at the mountains and then realise you've forgotten something. I tend to carry lots of spares in my van anyway, as when you're leading groups of people in the hills you can be certain that someone will have forgotten something.

Of course, it's going to depend on exactly what you've left behind as to what you can do next. If it's pouring down with rain and your waterproofs are back at home, then you're going to be stuck. But if you've forgotten your lunch box, that could be something a short drive to the shops might solve.

It's always worth asking around too, particularly if you find yourself in a busy car park. Mountain folk are generally nice folk and you'll be amazed at who might be able to lend you something.

I guess what I'm saying, is be careful and take a moment to discuss your choices. Don't think that just because you're there, you need to carry on without something you might regret not having with you. The mountains will always be there and having an enjoyable day in the future is better than having a miserable day today.

Running out of energy

Hopefully you'll have planned your day well enough and understand your own, and your groups, limitations for it to be a success, but you never know when something just might not feel right, and you don't think you can go any further. It could be sickness or just fatigue, but it's important to recognise it early.

Many mountain walks are out and back (or up and down) i.e., you take the same path to the summit that you'll return on, so if you find yourself struggling for pace or lacking energy halfway up, you need to stop and re-assess your plans. Abandoning your walk in favour of getting home safely is never a mistake. The mistake would be to continue on knowing you're running out of energy, putting yourself further away from your start point, and potentially making it more difficult to be rescued.

A note about energy drinks and gels. These are concentrated sources of energy that can assist you during an activity like mountain walking, but they're not a magic cure. I've used them a few times when I or a member of my group has been exhausted, but by the time you're at this stage you should already have a plan for getting down again. If you find yourself relying on them early in the day then it's definitely time to re-evaluate.

Motivation can also make a huge difference. If one of your group is really struggling, talking to them and keeping them positive can work miracles. Think about things you can do to encourage them to keep going.

Running out of time

Making sure you have enough time to complete your mountain walk is critical to your safety. I mention it a few times in this book but my number one tip for a successful mountain day is to start early. It gives you the best chance of completing your walk safely, in daylight, and also of beating any crowds.

All the walks in the back of this book (and all the mountain walking you should be doing as a beginner) are graded assuming you're walking in daylight. Trying to navigate in the mountains in the dark is an advanced skill, and without that skill, experience, and knowledge, it is highly dangerous.

Before setting out on any walk, be sure you know what time the sun will set where you are. It's really easy to find this information online by just searching for 'sunset time Brecon' for example. Many smartphone weather apps also have this information available. If you know what time it's going to get dark, you can plan your day around this.

If you find yourself in the mountains close to sunset or think, while you're out walking, that you're not going to get back to your car before sunset, take a moment to decide whether you need to change your plans and perhaps cut your walk short.

In Chapter 8, What to Take with You, I talk about carrying a headtorch. Once you start getting out more regularly, exploring for longer, or venturing out in the winter months, it's an absolute necessity. I routinely carry a couple of headtorches, plus spare batteries.

Getting lost

It happens to us all. Like many of the issues I've mentioned here, early recognition is key. If something doesn't feel right with your navigation, then check it as soon as

Carrying (and knowing how to read) a map is essential if you're walking somewhere you don't know well.

possible. Don't just keep going assuming it will fix itself. It may well do, but it's better to stop and be sure.

In Chapter 10, Navigation, I talk about how we split our walk into 'legs' between two control points (point A and point B), and how we use collecting features to 'tick off' along the way and catching features to let us know we've gone wrong. These are critical to ensuring we're going the right way and you must react if you hit a problem. The sooner you recognise you're not where you're supposed to be, the easier it will be to correct.

Try and retrace your steps, either on the map or on the ground. Find your last collecting feature or, if you've been thumbing the map, return to the last place that you were sure of your position. Hopefully this shouldn't be too far

Work together or ask other people. Assuming you're not on your own, discuss it with the rest of the group. Don't try and hide it as you could make things worse. Usually two (or more) heads are better than one. I regularly get stopped by walkers asking if they're in the right place and I'm always happy to help. It's very rare that somebody will just walk on by.

Use technology such as smartphone apps which can pinpoint your exact location and can display it on digital mapping, or give you an Ordnance Survey grid reference to locate yourself on your paper map.

When you get back on track, try to understand what you did wrong to get lost so that you don't make the same mistake again.

More experienced mountain folk will have learnt the art of relocating. They can look around at different features on the ground then match them to the map to pinpoint their location. This could be obvious things like roads, fence lines or rivers, or less obvious features such as changes in gradient or aspect of slope. However, these are advanced skills and require a great deal of practise.

Broken equipment

It's bound to happen at some point. No matter how well you look after your gear, one day, and probably at the worst possible time, something will break. Whether it's your kit or that of someone you're walking with, being able to perform simple repairs on the go can be really useful.

At the bottom of my rucksack, I have a mini MacGyver collection of bits that can be used to get me or my clients off the mountain. The repairs might not be glamorous and they're unlikely to last beyond the end of the day, but they'll serve a purpose.

Duct tape is the ultimate 'fixer' and can be used to repair everything from broken footwear to damaged zips. Find an old Tesco clubcard and wrap a good length of tape around it, or do the same around one of your walking poles or water bottles. This means you don't have to carry an actual roll of duct tape with you.

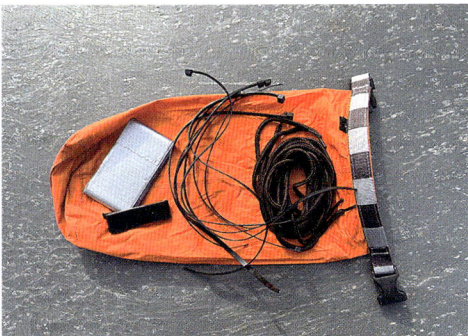

Cable ties can be used to keep a loose sole attached to a boot, mend broken rucksack straps or even as emergency laces.

Being able to perform simple repairs on the mountain can save your day.   *Photo: Andy Hewlett*

Cable ties can be used to keep a loose sole attached to a boot, mend broken rucksack straps or even as emergency laces.

Animals

Be thankful you're not walking through the Australian outback, otherwise this section could go on for pages. Wildlife in the UK mountains is very unlikely to do you any serious harm. Snakes and other small things that might bite are rare, and are usually far more afraid of you than you are of them. If you do see a snake sunbathing on the path in front of you, make a bit of noise and they'll happily slither away.

Farm animals are rarely that interested in you and would much rather get back to eating.

The author, a narrow path and a herd of cows. What could go wrong?

What you're far more likely to come across are farm animals, and it's the big ones that look the most scary. Dealing with cows isn't usually a problem. Stay away from them and they'll stay away from you. However, this can change when there are young calves around. All mothers are protective of their young, and cows have been known to be aggressive if they feel there's a threat. Give them a wide berth and you'll usually be fine. It's unlikely that you'll come across bulls in fields where there are public footpaths.

Dog walkers have been killed by stampeding cows. So, although it's essential that you keep your dog on a lead around farm animals, there is one notable exception. As difficult as it might seem, if you're walking with a dog and are being approached at speed by a herd of cows and can't escape easily, you must let go of your dog's lead. The cows will go after the dog (who will be much better at escaping the field than you) giving you a chance to get to safety. Thankfully this sort of thing is rare and, in my experience, walking tall and being brave is the way to deal with animals.

The biggest animal nuisance you're likely to experience in the mountains are midges, particularly in Scotland in the summer. Those tiny little biting buggers can ruin any mountain walk and there isn't really a whole lot you can do about them. You can wear a head net and you can spray yourself with various repellents, but I've never really found either guarantees your safety around a swarm. A windy day will stop them in their tracks, but your only real option is to go somewhere where they're not.

However, don't assume you're completely safe in England either. I remember belaying my climbing partner at the Roaches in the Peak District when, all of a sudden, a swarm of midges descended on me. I've never packed up and run off a climbing crag quite so quickly.

Ticks are another small, bitey nuisance. Unlike midges, however, ticks can cause a real problem as they have been known to carry Lyme disease. Usually found in long grass or on farm animals or pets, they can jump onto humans and spread disease. If you spot one, take care removing it. Many first aid kits contain a tick removal tool.

My best advice is to be careful walking through long grass, wear long trousers or gaiters, and keep an eye out for them on you and others. Tick buddy checks at the end of the day are good practice.

Blisters

Arghhh the dreaded blister! I must admit that I don't think we have the same problem today with blisters as we perhaps might have done a generation ago. Walking boots tend to be better designed and are more comfortable, and usually just feel right from the outset (we don't really need to 'wear boots in' like we used to have to).

All that aside, if you do get a blister on your mountain day, because you've borrowed a friend's pair of boots or just have soft skin, then they can be horrible.

The best treatment is early treatment. As soon as you feel something isn't quite right, stop and take action right away. The more you can do to protect the skin, the better chance you have of saving your day.

A traditional plaster can do the trick and it's likely most people will have them in their personal first aid kit. However, the ultimate product for blister relief is the Compeed Blister Plaster (own brand versions are also available from supermarkets and chemists). These pricey plasters have a gel cushion which provides instant pain relief and they also promote the healing process. If you're worried about blisters or have a history of them, it's definitely worth carrying a pack of these in your first aid kit.

Medical emergency

Whether something happens to you, or to one of your group, or you come across an injured party while out walking, being able to assist with a medical emergency is essential in a remote situation.

It's going to be impossible to teach you outdoor first aid in a few pages of this book, and I wouldn't even try. However, there are some basic life-saving tips that everyone should be aware of, whether you're wandering down your local high street or exploring the hills and mountains of the UK. The big difference between those two locations is that in your town centre, help will usually be with you in minutes, whereas in a remote mountain setting it will take much longer.

First aid training

I can't stress how important first aid training is. I believe it should be taught in schools and that everyone should have the opportunity to have some first aid training. Get in touch with your local branch of St John Ambulance or The British Red Cross Society to find out about how they can help. If you're a regular hill-walker, then I recommend a first aid course with an outdoor focus. These are available right across the country, and it's no exaggeration when I say they could save a life. Mountain professionals have to attend a two-day outdoor first aid course every three years, to ensure their skills are up to date.

Even in the optimum scenario, for example if you're able to get an immediate phone signal and the conditions are right for a helicopter rescue, it's still going to take considerably longer than the seven minutes that the NHS targets for ambulance response times in urban areas. In low cloud or poor weather, when a helicopter won't be able to reach you, it's not unusual for it to take several hours for a volunteer mountain rescue team to reach you.

Fortunately, first aid has got a lot simpler in recent years, with a much stronger emphasis on keeping a casualty comfortable while you seek professional help. I'll talk later in this chapter about the process for getting help (which should always be your first action).

Before approaching any casualty, be certain that it's safe for you to do so. If, for example, they've fallen halfway down a steep slope, it's probably better that you wait for people who know what they're doing, rather than risk you becoming a second casualty yourself. Be aware of things like falling rocks, loose ground or anything that can harm you. The temptation might be for you to rush in, but making sure the scene is safe should always be your number one priority.

If your casualty is not breathing then you need to get help immediately. This can simply be shouting for assistance. Shout loud and with purpose. You're trying to attract the attention of anyone that might be nearby, who hopefully has some first aid training.

In an ideal scenario, there'll be plenty of people around and someone will step up to start CPR. But what someone must be doing right from the outset is calling for help (read on for more on this). Hopefully, once you've got through to someone on the phone, they'll be able to lead you through what actions need to be taken.

If the casualty is conscious and breathing then they're much more likely to be able to tell you what's wrong, which takes a lot of the guesswork out of your diagnosis. In most situations all you're going to do is keep the casualty comfortable and summon help.

When we talk about keeping someone comfortable, we usually mean keeping them warm. Our bodies need heat to survive, and we can lose this quickly, particularly if we're at altitude, immobile and lying on the ground. If the casualty is lying down, and you're able to (without causing any pain or further harm), try to get something underneath them to protect them from the cold ground. Open their bag and get out any extra layers of clothing and do everything you can to keep them warm. Everyone should carry an emergency blanket of some sort in their rucksack, whether it's a cheap first aid product, an outdoor brand survival blanket or more professional bit of gear such as a Blizzard Bag.

Emergency thermal blankets like these cost around £1 and should be in everyone's rucksack.

A casualty being kept warm in a Blizzard Bag. Photo: Blizzard Protection Systems.

Put a hat on them (carefully), keep their hands warm, and do everything you can to make them comfortable.

Keeping a casualty warm might not always be what's required. For example, if some-one has seriously injured their leg and they're out in the open in the summer sun, you're going to need to keep them cool. You could erect a make-shift shelter to keep the sun off them, loosen their clothing and wet their lips.

Keeping a casualty comfortable also refers to keeping them mentally comfortable, so talk to them. It's important that they stay awake, and by keeping them in conversation you're helping monitor their condition and (hopefully) making them feel better.

If you need to deal with bleeding then the simple rule is to apply pressure directly to the wound. If you've got a sterile dressing in your personal first aid kit, that's great. Apply it directly to the wound. If there's more than one bleed or the blood soaks through your dressing, apply additional dressings on top. When you run out, use anything you can such as spare clothing to continue to apply pressure. If you're able, try to elevate the bleed.

If you suspect a sprain, or more seriously, a broken limb, more often than not you're going to have to keep the casualty comfortable until professional help arrives. You might be able to craft an emergency splint out of a walking pole but this sort of MacGyver-esque problem solving is usually best left to those who know what they're doing.

As with any medical emergency, if you're at all unsure then seek proper medical assistance.

Calling for help

If the situation is looking beyond your skill set, it's time to call for help. In the UK we're very lucky to have an amazing network of mountain rescue services who can help with everything from providing support and navigation assistance over the phone, to arranging evacuation to hospital.

Mountain rescue services in the UK are staffed by volunteers who all have normal lives, and typically, full-time jobs. Depending on your location, it can take several hours from your initial phone call to help arriving. So, if you're able to get a casualty off the mountain yourself without causing any further damage, then that can often be a better option. Of course, if you're at all unsure and genuinely need help then never hesitate in calling.

If you come across a casualty, or if you have a problem with a member of your group, or if you become injured yourself, take a minute to assess the situation before rushing

A large team of mountain rescue volunteers carrying a casualty to safety.   *Photo: Rich Griffiths*

to call 999. If someone has fallen over and twisted their ankle and you're a group of rugby players 50m away from the car park, then assisting the casualty down to a better location can make things a lot easier. From the car park you can decide whether you can get the casualty to hospital yourselves or call for a regular ambulance – all of which will happen much quicker than if you need to call out mountain rescue.

Of course, if the situation is serious, especially if you're dealing with a life-or-death situation, then getting help to you ASAP is critical. It's time to call out the mountain rescue services. There are a few important steps you should follow:

Step One – Where are you?

Before calling for help, you need to know exactly where you are. Saying you're on 'Snowdon' is not going to help the emergency services find you. Try to give a detailed description of your location for example 'We're climbing Snowdon on the Llanberis path in between the Halfway Station and Halfway House'. Even better (and what you should be aspiring to) is an accurate, Ordnance Survey six-figure grid reference e.g., SH 598 571, or better still a full grid reference such as SH 59802 571976. This will pinpoint your location to a 1m² area, which is perfect.

If you're not yet a competent map reader, you can get the OS grid reference for your exact location using smartphone apps like OS Locate or OSMaps. These don't rely on having a phone signal and can quickly pinpoint your exact position anywhere in the UK. Do be sure to give them a few seconds to accurately locate you, particularly if you don't have a good line of sight to the sky (which is where the satellites are!)

Newer services are also becoming more common such as What3Words, which has cleverly divided the whole world in to three-metre squares and given each square a unique combination of three words, such as ///tinned.prompts.juggled. This might look like gibberish to you and me but anyone using the What3Words website can tap in those three words and see exactly where you are. Emergency services are very familiar with this technology and it can be a great way to get help fast. You can download the What3Words app for your smartphone from your device's app store.

Mountain rescue teams also have their own technology for locating casualties, so don't worry if you're struggling to pinpoint your location.

Step Two – Gather some basic information

The emergency services will ask you some important questions which are essential for allocating the right resources to best help you. If you have all this information written down in advance, it will speed up their response and save valuable mobile phone battery life. You may also find you have to come away from a casualty to get a phone signal, so having everything to hand will save you running back and forth.

Try to collate and write down the following information:

- Your exact location from step one above.

- Exactly what's happened. Who is injured (their approximate age, general condition, etc). How they're injured. What position they're in right now. Do they have any medical conditions? What they're wearing. If you're first aid trained and can give more information about the casualty's condition, then even better.

- If you're in a group, what is the make-up of the rest of your party? Are they in a safe place? Do they need assistance too? Is everyone warm and dry?

Mountain professionals and those trained in first aid will carry a blank 'casualty report form' often printed on rugged waterproof paper. This acts as a prompt for the sort of information you need to gather before calling for help. An example can be found in the appendix.

Step Three – Call for help

Dial 999 and ask for the police and then mountain rescue. In the UK, police control centres liaise with mountain rescue services to arrange help and they'll be well used to people calling with mountain emergencies. They'll ask you for all the information you've gathered during steps one and two above.

If you don't have a phone signal, you may need to relocate from where the casualty is. Your phone will route 999 calls through any available network so do keep trying, even if you don't think your own network has service. Be sensible about your battery life from now on as you may need it again, particularly if you're on your own near the end of a day when your phone might be running low.

Emergency SMS

You can also send a text message to the emergency services using the emergencySMS system. You need to register your phone in advance of your day by simply texting the word 'register' to 999 and then follow the prompts. Then, when you need help you send a structured text message to 999, such as 'police/mountain rescue - 60yr old male hiker suffering heart attack – SH 59802 571976'. This service is great when you have little or no phone signal or are desperately low on battery life, as sending and receiving SMS messages uses considerably less of both. Although originally setup by BT for use by deaf, hard of hearing and speech-impaired people, the service works brilliantly in these scenarios. Search the Internet for 'emergencySMS' to find out more.

If your phone is dead or broken or lost, or you don't have one with you, then you're going to need to think differently. Depending on the level of the emergency you may find yourself having to leave the casualty on their own while you go for help. Ideally, you'd aim to leave someone with the casualty and send two or more people to get assistance, but this may not always be possible. If you're leaving someone injured, they're going to get cold quickly so make sure they're as warm and comfortable as you can get them. If they're unconscious, consider leaving a note in an obvious place, in case someone else stumbles across them while you're gone.

We're really getting into quite unusual territory now. As a new walker, I think it's unlikely that you're going to be somewhere very remote on your own and a long way from a good mobile signal. Although it shouldn't be relied upon, you'll be amazed at how good the reception is on your phone – certainly while using the routes at the back of this book.

A casualty being looked after by mountain rescue volunteers.

Photo: Rich Griffiths.

Step Four – Look after the casualty

Remember that, unlike calling for an ambulance to your home, workplace or your local town centre, mountain rescue will take some time to get to you, and this could be several hours. After your initial emergency call, mountain rescue volunteers typically assemble at a central location to get their gear together and then need to make their way to you. If you're a long way from a road, this can take time. You need to make sure that you, the casualty and everyone in your group is safe, warm and dry. If you're not moving around or the casualty is lying on the floor, they will get cold very quickly so use all your spare clothing and emergency equipment to prioritise those most in need.

Keep talking to the casualty, whether you think they can hear you or not, and keep your own spirits up whichever way you can. If you have a good phone signal and plenty of battery life, the emergency call operators will try to stay with you to give you first aid advice until the medical professionals arrive.

When rescue arrives

Help may arrive in a number of ways. It could be another walker coming along with more first aid training than you, or even a doctor who might be out enjoying the countryside themselves. Part of dealing with a casualty is dealing with other people too, so if you need help from passer's by, be sure to ask for it. Equally if there are enough people already dealing with the incident you don't want a crowd forming.

The help you've called will probably arrive in the form of volunteers from the local mountain rescue team. It could be a whole bunch of them, or more likely a smaller forward party who have made their way to you quickly while the rest of the team follows. The team leader will immediately take charge of the incident, but don't walk away as they'll want to know as much as possible about what's happened from you, particularly if the casualty is not able to communicate themselves.

If a helicopter arrives on scene before mountain rescue volunteers, you'll need to make it obvious that it's you that needs the help, particularly if there are lots of people around. Don't simply wave, but raise your arms up to make a 'Y' shape. The pilot will recognise this as the universal distress signal. The large red and white Coastguard helicopters produce a huge amount of downdraft so be aware of this. Secure loose items, even as large as rucksacks, as these can be moved around quite easily. Either tie them together or sit someone on them. Stow away any emergency shelter you might have been using and remove hats. If you see a winch cable coming towards you, do not attempt to grab it. There'll be a person on the end of it who will be very capable and know exactly what they're doing, so just let them do their thing.

A casualty being winched into an HM Coastguard helicopter.

Photo: Nick Read

Learning essential skills such as map reading will make you a more competent outdoor person.

17 Where Can I Learn More?

This book covers what you need to know to climb your first mountain, but there is no substitute for practical experience. The theory suddenly makes a lot more sense when you try it out for real.

Fortunately, there are some great courses that can guide you in your early steps.

Skills courses from Mountain Training

Mountain Training is the UK awarding body for qualifications in walking, climbing and mountaineering. While most of their work is training outdoor leaders, back in 2014 they recognised there was also a need for personal skills courses and introduced the Hill Skills and Mountain Skills courses. These are designed to help you stay safe and enjoy your time outdoors, and aim to equip you with the basic knowledge and safety skills required to participate in hill and mountain walking in your own time.

Hill Skills

The Hill Skills course is your key to getting started in countryside walking. No previous hill walking experience is required to attend a Hill Skills course because the content of the course is aimed at beginners. If you do have some experience of hill walking but aren't confident about planning walks, navigating and understanding the equipment required, then the Hill Skills course is an ideal way to learn.

Mountain Skills

The Mountain Skills course is an ideal choice for walkers interested in transferring their walking skills to steep, remote or more mountainous terrain. Ideally, participants will have some basic hill walking experience and have a reasonable level of fitness. Courses are run in the higher mountain areas of the UK and Ireland.

The syllabus for both courses covers how to successfully plan a walk in the UK or Ireland, what things should you consider while out walking and what can make life easier, how being suitably dressed and equipped can make the difference between a great day out and a complete disaster, and how the weather affects the hills and mountains on your day out. You'll also look at navigation, including everything from selecting a compass to navigation strategies and an intro to GPS, cover environmental knowledge such as how to minimise your impact on the hill and information on good practice and useful organisations, as well as how to respond to any hazards you encounter and what to do in an emergency.

The Hill Skills and Mountain Skills courses are nationally accredited and developed by Mountain Training. They are widely available and are delivered by approved course providers and tutors who are all experienced Mountain Training qualification holders. The courses typically take place over two days (often at weekends) and are available right across the UK and Ireland.

Visit *www.mountain-training.org* to find an upcoming course near you.

Navigator Awards from the National Navigation Award Scheme

If you're already familiar with the outdoors but your navigation skills sometimes let you down, I'd highly recommend the Bronze, Silver and Gold Navigator Awards from the National Navigation Award Scheme (NNAS). Set up as a registered charity to promote the teaching of land navigation skills through its Navigator Awards, their popular courses transform your outdoor skills over just a weekend. The focus is on practical navigation and encouraging people of all ages into the outdoors. Founded in 1994 by teacher and orienteer Peter Palmer, the organisation has gone from strength to strength and has guided thousands of people through the progressive award structure to become confident navigators.

A Mountain Skills course can introduce you to more adventurous terrain.

The NNAS is a personal performance scheme for all ages to learn navigation skills and gain the confidence to get out and enjoy the countryside. Their Navigator Awards give lovers of the outdoors, whatever their sport, age or fitness, the freedom to explore the paths, trails, hills and mountains of Britain. Progress through the Bronze, Silver and Gold Awards to take you from being an absolute map and compass novice to become an expert navigator.

The awards have been adopted by Duke of Edinburgh Award groups, military cadet groups, Scouts and Guides and many other youth groups, as well as by individuals wishing to develop their own navigation skills. Having proven navigation skills is also a requirement for professional outdoor qualifications and membership of mountain and lowland rescue organisations.

Bronze Navigator Award

On the Bronze Navigator Award, you'll cover essential map reading skills and learn how to use 'handrail features', like paths and walls, to guide you along your way, as well as learning how to measure distance, understand grid references and plan your own routes. You'll also learn the basics of how to use a compass and how to use it with your map to ensure you don't get lost. The Bronze Award will take you from relying on friends or guidebooks to being able to plan a walk and follow it successfully.

Learning new map skills on a National Navigation Award Scheme Bronze Navigator course.

Silver Navigator Award

On the Silver Navigator Award, you'll start to leave the paths behind and navigate in open country using a compass on short bearings. As your confidence increases, you'll learn more advanced compass skills and add timing and pacing into the mix. The Silver Award takes place on more difficult terrain than the Bronze Award and away from easy-to-follow paths and trails.

The Gold Navigator Award

The Gold Navigator Award is the industry leading navigation qualification for those really looking to push their boundaries. You'll hone your skills developed during the Bronze and Silver Awards and discover new techniques to help you navigate in the most complex terrain. Even in poor visibility, the Gold Navigator will be able to follow a route with ease and confidence.

Visit *www.nnas.org.uk* to find an upcoming course near you.

A qualified Mountain Leader at work on Crib Goch in Eryri (Snowdonia).

18 Hiring a Mountain Guide

If you're at all unsure about your first serious mountain adventure and you haven't been persuaded by everything I've written here, then I'd highly recommend paying a professional to look after you. They will know the area where you want to walk, can provide a safe pair of hands and will take all the guesswork out of your day – and it might not cost as much you think.

Mountain guides make their living from doing just that – guiding people in the mountains. They will offer all sorts of services from simple guided hikes to scrambling days out or serious rock climbing and mountaineering adventures. The businesses offering guiding services range from small, one-man bands to larger operations employing multiple guides.

In the UK, anyone can call themselves a 'mountain guide' (with a small 'g') and offer to take you into the hills (unlike in the Alps where it is a regulated profession restricted to IFMGA Mountain Guides). However, you really want to be looking for someone who is qualified and experienced, if you're going to put your life in their hands. You wouldn't use an unqualified driving instructor to teach you how to drive or let a complete novice cut your hair, so why skimp on finding the right mountain guide where there's potential

A Mountain Leader keeping a group safe on Yr Wyddfa (Snowdon).   *Photo: Tom Swinhoe.*

for greater risk. Properly qualified mountain guides will also have insurance and under-take regular outdoor first aid training

Mountain Training is the organisation that manages qualifications in walking, climbing and mountaineering in the UK. It's responsible for the training and assessment of people who look after other people in these environments, whether that's leading a walk in the mountains, coaching in a climbing wall or teaching rock climbing. People who hold Mountain Training qualifications have been assessed at a nationally agreed standard.

There are a number of qualifications suited to leading individuals and groups walking in the hills, but the one you want to look out for is the Mountain Leader award. Outdoor leaders who hold this award will have gone through rigourous training and assessment, with a lengthy period of consolidation in between. They have to prove their leadership experience and should keep up to date with the industry through regular personal development, so you be certain that those who have reached this standard have been well trained and assessed. When looking around for a mountain guide, be sure they have their Mountain Leader qualification as a minimum.

Of course, you'll come across people who have more, and higher, qualifications such as the Winter Mountain Leader, International Mountain Leader, Mountaineering and

Climbing Instructor awards or even a BMG / IFMGA Mountain Guide. What holders of these awards have in common is that they all hold the Mountain Leader award or its equivalent too, but their further qualifications enable them to lead groups in winter conditions, in mountainous regions outside of the UK and on serious summer and winter climbs.

There are a few ways you can find a suitably qualified guide. The Mountain Training website maintains a public database of qualified outdoor instructors. You can access this database online by searching for 'Mountain Training – find a leader'. From this website you'll be able to filter for 'Mountain Leader' in 'North Wales', for example, after which you'll be presented with a list of outdoor professionals who have asked to be included in the database. You'll be able to view the public profile for each person which will tell you more about their qualifications, experience, CPD (continued personal development) and most importantly their contact details.

The downside of the database is, assuming you're looking for a guide in a mountainous region (as opposed to Central London), it's likely to return pages and pages of results, seemingly in no useful order. A better option perhaps, would be to use your favourite Internet search engine and then crosscheck the results with the Mountain Training database. A simple search using words such as 'Ben Nevis mountain guide' will return an abundance of shiny outdoor professionals' websites. Spend some time reading what they have to offer, have a look for previous client testimonials and then get in touch. In my experience mountain guides are nearly always 'people people' and will love chatting to you, finding out about what you're after and giving you the best advice.

In recent years the prevalence of Facebook Groups means there are now clusters of like-minded people online who will happily share reviews and feedback of people they've met and / or worked with in the mountains. Try searching Facebook for 'Peak District walking groups' for example. Mention what you're hoping to get from your mountain day and sit back and watch the recommendations come flooding in.

Finally, the age-old method of word of mouth can rarely be topped. Ask around in the office, drop it in to conversation or mention it to friends and family. You never know who might have already climbed your target mountain and may be able to recommend a guide to work with.

There will inevitably be a cost associated with hiring a mountain guide, but it might not be as expensive as you think. As with most industries, you'll often pay more for the highest qualified people, but if you're looking for someone to take you up Scafell Pike,

Hiring a professional can get you to places you might not be able to reach on your own.

do you really need an Everest summiter? While they'll have some great stories to share with you on your day, they're likely to be more expensive than a typical Mountain Leader.

It's also worth checking that whoever you choose to work with has their own public liability insurance and has an up to date outdoor first aid qualification. They should be able to provide certificates for both of these without issue and may even have them available to look at on their websites. While technically neither is mandatory, I'd be wary of hiring the services of a guide who doesn't have them.

19 Popular Mountain Challenges

If you're looking for something to aspire to (or maybe you've already signed up to one and that's why you've bought this book), there are several popular UK mountain challenges. These are definitely a big step up from the beginner routes in the back of this book, and absolutely not recommended without some prior hillwalking experience, a good amount of physical training and, in most cases, a professional guide. However, they are something you can aim for in the future.

Trail 100's

I've already mentioned *Trail Magazine's* 'definitive collection of the 100 UK peaks all hillwalkers must climb' earlier in the book, and while it isn't perhaps a recognised challenge as such, it's definitely something you could aspire to. There's no time limit to this one, just a collection of the best mountain summits hand-picked by the experts at *Trail Magazine*. Now imagine if you were able to tick off all 100?

The mighty Ben Nevis is the usual starting point for the National Three Peaks challenge.   *Photo: Tom Swinhoe*

National Three Peaks

The original, and best known, UK mountain challenge involves climbing the highest mountains in Scotland, England and Wales in 24 hours, usually from north to south. This is not only physically challenging, in that you're going to have to summit Ben Nevis at 1,345m (4,413ft), Scafell Pike at 978m (3,209ft) and Yr Wyddfa (Snowdon) at 1,085m (3,560ft), but also logistically, as you need to get yourself from the Scottish Highlands, through the English Lake District and down to North Wales. For some time now the mountaineering community has been less keen on promoting the 24-hour challenge for obvious environmental reasons. The reality is you'll spend as much time being driven up and down featureless motorways as you will exploring the mountains – often in the dark. An increasingly popular alternative is tackling the challenge over a long weekend. It's far more reasonable to make your way up to Fort William on a Friday, spend the night in local accommodation and climb Ben Nevis first thing on the Saturday morning. After lunch you make your way to the Lake District, spending the night there before taking on Scafell Pike first thing Sunday morning. This is followed by the shorter drive to North Wales, to finish with Yr Wyddfa (Snowdon) on Sunday afternoon. This even allows you time to get home on Sunday evening so you can be back at work on Monday. Doing it this way means you might only need one day off work, and you'll get two good night's sleep while supporting local businesses by using their accommodation. Of course, there are still environmental considerations in driving many hundreds of miles, but car sharing and spreading it over a weekend might help reduce the impact, if only a little.

A group of walkers on Pen-y-Ghent at the beginning of their Yorkshire Three Peaks challenge.

The National Three Peaks challenge has been completed by many and in some quite unusual ways. Successful attempts have been recorded of people climbing each mountain and then cycling, and even walking, to the next one or completing the National, Yorkshire, and Welsh, Three Peaks challenges in one go!

Yorkshire Three Peaks

The Yorkshire Three Peaks challenge is nearly becoming as popular as the National Three Peaks. However, it is more achievable for most people, principally as it doesn't require driving hundreds of miles between mountains. It is still definitely a challenge, involving walking 38.6km (24 miles) with over 1,585m (5,200ft) of ascent climbing Pen-y-ghent, Whernside and Ingleborough. This is usually done in under 12 hours (although the record is under two-and-a-half hours). The usual start and finish is in the normally peaceful village of Horton in Ribblesdale, with its plentiful parking and numerous campsites. The route is fairly easy to follow, but if you're tackling it on one of the mid-summer weekends you needn't worry too much about navigation, as you'll probably be in a procession of hundreds taking on the same challenge, often as part of charity events.

The Yorkshire Dales National Park Authority have created a smartphone app for the Yorkshire Three Peaks Challenge; profits from the sale of which contribute towards the huge cost of path repair. Look for it in your device's app store.

Heading up the magnificent Cadair Idris, one of the Welsh Three Peaks.

Welsh Three Peaks

A relative newcomer to mountain challenges, the Welsh Three Peaks challenge sees you climbing Snowdon in the north, Cadair Idris in mid-Wales and Pen y Fan in the south. This is also usually completed in less than 24 hours, with a total walking distance of 27.4km (17 miles) and an impressive 2,334m (7,657ft) of climbing. The driving time between each mountain is much more reasonable than the National Three Peaks and it's quite possible to complete the challenge in one day in the height of summer.

Welsh 3,000's

Not for amateurs, this challenge is a big step up from the ones you've already read about. Challengers need to reach the top of all 15 of Wales' 3,000ft mountains within 24 hours and without using any transport, walking a total distance of over 30 miles. Often completed by fell runners, it can be done by walking but it's extremely tough going and only suitable for very fit and experienced mountain walkers. The terrain is rocky and navigation is difficult, and may even require bivvying at the top of Yr Wyddfa (Snowdon) the night before. A real challenge and one not to be underestimated.

When you're ready to be a bit more adventurous.

20 What Next?

If you're already looking ahead to your next mountain adventure, you might be wondering how you can step things up a gear. What I love about climbing mountains is that there is something out there for everyone. There are great 'beginner hills' for those who've never climbed anything, and then there are serious mountain experiences waiting for you when you're ready.

The important thing is that you take your mountain climbing progression at your own pace. If you quickly feel confident with smaller hills, then you can start looking at more exciting mountain adventures. Take your time and build up your mountain experience steadily.

If you feel you're ready to move on, here are some other mountainy things to try.

Scrambling

This is the 'grey area' between hill walking and rock climbing. Even on the simplest Grade I scrambles you're likely to need to use your hands at some point, and it's possible you'll experience exposure (i.e. big drops!). At the top end, Grade III scrambles are essentially moderate rock climbs. Scrambling is definitely a step up from walking and should be approached with care due to the added risks involved.

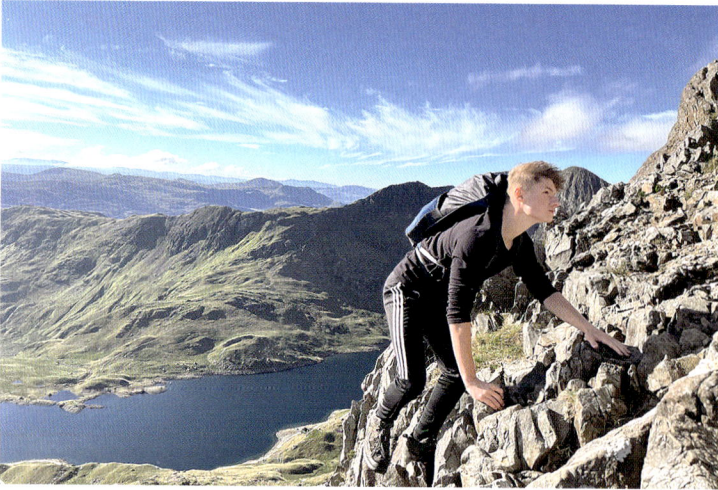

Enjoying a first scrambling adventure on Crib Goch.

Route finding on scrambles can be challenging. It's unlikely you'll be following a traditional 'path' and more often than not you're simply following your nose. If you don't think your nose is up to it then consider hiring a mountain guide (see Chapter 18, Hiring a Mountain Guide). There are scrambling guide books available but don't expect them to provide step-by-step instructions.

There will be occasions while scrambling when you need to downclimb. This can be scary for beginners and should be taken with care. Most of my scrambling is up stuff!

While you don't necessarily need any special equipment for simple Grade I scrambles, you might want to consider whether a helmet would be appropriate for protecting against falling rocks from above. When you're moving up to Grade III scrambles then you're likely to need a climbing harness, ropes and a good knowledge of rock climbing.

Some popular UK scrambles are:

The (in)famous Crib Goch arête on Yr Wyddfa (Snowdon). Here you'll find yourself climbing up from the Pyg Track, onto the narrow ridge where the exposure is very real, with huge drops either side of you. Also in Wales is the North Ridge of Tryfan - another fantastic Grade I scramble, where route finding is tricky, and you can easily head off course onto dangerous rock climbing territory.

In the Lake District you'll find Striding Edge up onto Helvellyn, a decent sized ridge walk with mostly easy moves, but one nerve-wracking downclimb.

Scotland is home to some of the best scrambling in the country from the Carn Mor Dearg arête on Ben Nevis to the big days out in the Cuillin on Skye.

Rock climbing and abseiling in the Peak District.

If you'd like to experience the excitement of scrambling but with the safety of a qualified and experienced mountain guide, I'd definitely recommend attending a scrambling course. Use your favourite online search engine to look for 'intro to scrambling' or similar and you'll find a variety of one, two, or multi-day courses aimed at all abilities.

Rock climbing

If, while you've been out mountain walking, you've heard the jangling of metal around you or spotted brightly coloured people hanging off a crag ahead of you, that's rock climbing.

This is a sport that should definitely only be attempted under the supervision of qualified and experienced instructors. For one thing you'll need a lot of gear, starting with a climbing harness, special footwear, a helmet, ropes and a climbing rack (the gear you use to protect you on your climb).

Rock climbing isn't for everyone and there's no expectation that you'll move from mountain walking into rock climbing. In fact, they are quite different sports and while most rock climbers will also be mountain walkers (you need to walk to the crags), it's certainly not the case that most mountain walkers are rock climbers.

If you are interested in getting started, check locally for an indoor climbing wall. Traditionally used in the winter by climbers trying to get out of the cold, indoor climbing centres are now hugely popular all year round and are used by all sorts of people. Most offer 'intro to climbing' courses for beginners and will often help match you up with other climbers of a similar ability looking for partners.

Climbing a mountain to see the sunrise is an increasingly popular activity.

When you're ready, you can then move outdoors to try your hand at sport climbing (where bolts are fixed in the rock for you to clip into – a bit like indoors) or trad climbing where you'll need to place your own protection into cracks in the rock, using gear like nuts and cams.

Walking at night

Climbing a mountain in the dark is a very different experience and not for everybody, but if you're a bit more confident and you plan properly, it can be amazing.

For example, watching the sun rise from a summit in the early hours of a summer morning or seeing it set in the evening is stunning.

You obviously need to take great care when walking in the dark, and you'll need to be certain about your navigation skills if you're not being guided. Things will look very different and considerably more challenging without daylight.

Winter walking

As I mentioned earlier in the book, climbing mountains in winter is a very different ball game. The risks are much greater than summer walking and you'll need extra gear, you'll need to be considerably fitter and should have some training in how to walk in winter.

Fortunately, winter skills courses are a popular activity offered by a variety of providers. Apologies to my North Wales and Lake District colleagues, but for the best winter skills

Conditions when climbing mountains in winter are very different to the rest of the year and require additional training and experience.

experience you really need to head up to Scotland. This gives you the optimal chance of good winter conditions (i.e., snow) which unfortunately is more difficult to predict south of the border.

Many providers offer weekend (two-day) and longer, five-day courses. If you're fit enough and can get the time off work (and have the money), I recommend opting for the five-day course. They often run side by side with everyone starting together and then the short course attendees leave at the end of day two, forlorn that they're not carrying on for another three days.

Winter skills courses focus on the fundamentals, including: personal movement (how to walk in crampons, how to kick and cut steps), using an ice axe and how to self-arrest (stop yourself if you slip on a slope), winter navigation, avalanche avoidance and generally getting to grips with the winter environment.

Over a longer course you'll have lots of opportunities to practise, refine your techniques and put your new skills to good use. Winter skills courses are designed to give you the confidence and knowledge to go hill walking safely in winter conditions.

I should also point out that they're great fun.

Use your favourite search engine to look for 'Scottish winter skills courses'. Mention it to a loved one as they make great birthday / Christmas gift ideas.

The author enjoying winter climbing in Eryri (Snowdonia).   *Photo: Andy Hewlett*

Wild camping / bothying

What do you do if you want to climb a really big mountain, or perhaps more than one, and there isn't enough time in the day? You stay out overnight of course.

Wild camping

Wild camping is the term used for pitching your tent overnight, anywhere other than a formal campsite. This is an increasingly popular activity with adventurers but it's not without its problems. Wild camping is generally accepted and shouldn't be confused with 'fly camping', a more recent phenomenon when people setup camp close to the road, make lots of noise and often leave all their equipment and rubbish behind.

Technically, wild camping is not permitted in most of England and Wales without prior permission from the landowner or farmer. All land is owned by someone and you should have their permission to wild camp on it. However, it is widely accepted that wild camping is OK when following a few basic rules.

Trail Magazine, the popular hillwalking and hiking magazine have produced a handy wild camping code:

- Camp high on open hills, away from main tracks, houses and farms.

- Minimise numbers of people and tents.

- Pitch your camp late in the evening and leave early in the morning.

- Don't dig drainage ditches, trample plants or move rocks.

- If asked by a landowner to move on, do so respectfully and without argument.

- Don't light any fires; use a proper camping stove for cooking.

- Toileting should be well away from any water source or path (30m or more).

- Paper and sanitary items should be bagged up and carried out, not buried.

- Do not use streams or rivers for washing with soaps or detergent.

- Maintain the peace by aiming to be as quiet as possible during your camp.

- Don't remain in the same spot for more than two nights maximum.

- Bag up and carry out all litter, including food scraps.

- Leave no trace that you've camped.

Bothying

A bothy is typically a basic shelter found in remote locations, and of hugely varying degrees of quality. It could just be four walls and a roof or it might have some kitchen facilities and maybe even some beds. They're often provided free of charge on a first come – first served basis. It's for this reason that I usually tell people planning to spend the night in a bothy that they should take a tent or shelter and assume they're going to have to use it. If there is space in the bothy when they arrive, that's a bonus.

I've arrived at a remote bothy with friends in the early evening, made dinner and settled in for the night only to be joined by another group just as we were getting ready for bed. Suddenly everything got a bit cosier!

There are bothies that you can book in advance. Check out the Mountain Bothies Association to find out more.

Trail running

If you're a super fit running machine then you might consider branching out into trail running. Also known as mountain or fell running (fell being a term used in the Lake District), this is the sport of running off-road and appears to be booming in popularity. You can run on your own, with a club or take part in one of the numerous organised events all over the country.

Climbing mountains abroad

This book focuses on climbing mountains in the UK because, as a beginner that's where you're likely to be starting. But it's a big world out there and if you're loving what we have in this country, you're really going to love what the rest of the planet has to offer.

You don't necessarily need a huge amount of experience to climb some amazing mountains, especially if you go with an organised group. Big adventure travel companies such as Explore, Exodus Travels or Much Better Adventures all operate mountain climbing adventures across the globe, aimed at relative beginners. Smaller operations such as Mountain Expeditions or the LGBTQ+ friendly Pride Expeditions are run by professional mountaineers, and while their holiday choice might be more limited, their mountain knowledge cannot be matched.

Some great 'starter' international climbs include Triglav, Slovenia's highest mountain at 2,864m (9,396ft) which can be tackled in just two days. Or head to Morocco and climb Toubkal, the highest peak in the Atlas Mountains, and the highest point in North Africa.

A group of hikers in Nepal trekking to Everest Base Camp.

At 4,167m (13,671ft) it can also be climbed in as little as a couple of days. Staying in Africa, the highest point on the continent is Kilimanjaro at 5,895m (19,341ft). This is a much bigger affair that takes a minimum of seven days to summit. I would advise a longer acclimatisation period as it is high enough for potentially fatal high altitude mountain sickness to develop. The rule of thumb is one day for every thousand feet above 10,000 feet. The more responsible guides insist on climbing a lower peak first to acclimatise, before tackling Kilimanjaro.

In Asia, reaching Everest Base Camp in Nepal at 5,365m (17,598ft) is on many people's bucket lists, but this is definitely a more committing hike, usually requiring a couple of weeks.

Nearer home, but certainly a big challenge is Mont Blanc. The highest point in Western Europe at 4,808m (15,774ft) is typically climbed in three days but will require a strong level of fitness, good winter movement skills and, realistically, at least a few days at altitude beforehand in order to acclimatise.

As with all international mountain climbing, try to experience more than just the climb. Spend time (and money) in the towns and villages, and learn more about the countries you're visiting. Many of these areas are not wealthy and rely solely on adventure tourism for their income.

Route Maps and Guides

Taking in the view on the Pyg Track (Route 8).

Grindsbrook Clough in the Peak District with the Mam Tor ridge visible in the background.

21 Route Maps and Guides

If you've read this book from the beginning, then you're ready to venture out into the mountains and aim for your first summit. Over the coming pages you'll find detailed route maps and guides to what I believe are some of our most popular and achievable hill and mountain walks. I've tried my best to choose a selection from around the country, so hopefully you won't have to travel too far. However, the very make-up of the UK means that if you live in the South East of England, then you're going to need to make a weekend of it.

All the routes in this book are designed for beginners who may not have any more outdoor experience than simply reading this book. The routes mostly follow marked footpaths which should make for simple navigation and are all popular with walkers, so it's unlikely you're ever going to be on your own. Feel free to photograph the relevant pages with your phone, as they are for your personal use.

Locations

Locations (for where a walk starts from) used in the route guides are provided in three different formats which offer varying degrees of accuracy. Always check before setting off that you know exactly where you're heading to.

Royal Mail Post Codes

Example: LL55 4TU

Post codes are the least reliable method for pinpointing a location – particularly in the mountains. A post code in a town centre might cover ten properties all within a 100m radius, whereas post codes in rural areas typically cover the same number of properties but over a much larger area. Use a post code in your sat nav or Google Maps to help you plan your journey but be aware it's unlikely to be spot on.

OS Grid References

Example: SH 583 598

I've included six-figure Ordnance Survey grid references which, as you'll know from reading the navigation chapter, give you a 100m^2 area. Much more accurate than a post code but you will need to understand how OS grid references work … and have an OS map. If you're using the OSMaps app on your smartphone, then you can input the grid references there for a pretty accurate location.

What3Words Location

Example: ///shady.ground.joys

The most accurate but least used method is What3Words, whose technology has divided the world into three-metre squares and given each square a unique combination of three words. Extremely simple to use and understand. Access the What3Words website or download the smartphone app.

Walk grades

I've given each route a grade; either **EASY**, **MODERATE** or **HARD**. The problem with walk grades is that they're very subjective. What's easy for one person might be hard for another. However, as this book and the routes in it are aimed at absolute beginners and those who are unlikely to have climbed a mountain before, I've taken that into account. Expect an **EASY** route to be relatively short, reasonably simple to navigate, with little risk of falling off the side of a mountain. A **MODERATE** walk might involve covering a greater distance, so you're likely to be walking for longer, may require some extra concentration when navigating and the route could have you walking near some steep edges. A **HARD** walk will be a longer day out in the mountains with perhaps more exposed walking and big drops. But all are within the ability of a 'beginner'. It goes without saying that all the routes involve a fair amount of uphill walking!

EASY

Route 1 – Cat Bells 451m (1,480ft) – A great 'starter' hill in the Lake District.

Route 2 – Mam Tor 517m (1,696ft) – The Peak District's most popular peak.

Route 3 – Pen y Fan 886m (2,907ft) – The highest peak in South Wales but achievable by most.

Route 4 – Pen-y-ghent 694m (2,277ft) – Another great introduction to mountain climbing, found in the Yorkshire Dales.

Route 5 – Roseberry Topping 320m (1,049ft) – Everyone's favourite North Eastern hill.

MODERATE

Route 6 – Yes Tor and High Willhays 621m (2,039ft) – The highest point on Dartmoor.

Route 7 – Yr Wyddfa (Snowdon) via the Llanberis Path 1,085m (3,560ft) – The most popular and 'easiest' route up Wales' highest mountain.

Route 8 – Yr Wyddfa (Snowdon) via the Pyg / Miners' Tracks 1,085m (3,560ft) – Some argue it's quicker, it's certainly shorter, but you'll definitely have to work a bit harder.

HARD

Route 9 – Ben Nevis via the Mountain Track 1,345m (4,413ft) – The highest point in the UK and surely the ultimate mountain day out.

Route 10 – Cadair Idris 893m (2,930ft) – The highest point in mid-Wales and a challenging day out.

Route 11 – Scafell Pike from Wasdale 978m (3,209ft) England's highest peak, found in the heart of the Lake District.

Route 1   **Cat Bells, Lake District National Park**
Start / Finish CA12 5UE or NY 246 211 or ///noisy.curtains.tutorial

Route 2   **Mam Tor, Peak District National Park, Derbyshire**
Start /Finish S33 8WH or SK 149 830 or ///hydration.best.gender

Route 3   **Pen y Fan, South Wales**
Start / Finish LD3 8NL or SN 983 203 or ///encourage.extreme.autumn

Route 4   **Pen-y-ghent, Yorkshire Dales National Park**
Start / Finish BD24 0HF or SD 808 726 or ///covertly.overture.cloak

Route 5   **Roseberry Topping, North York Moors National Park**
Start / Finish TS9 6QS or NZ 570 128 or ///trimmer.configure.expand

Route 6   **Yes Tor and High Willhays, Dartmoor National Park**
Start / Finish EX20 4LU or SX 561 918 or ///cross.sung.printout

Route 7   **Yr Wyddfa (Snowdon) via the Llanberis Path**
Start / Finish LL55 4TU or SH 583 598 or ///shady.ground.joys

Route 8   **Yr Wyddfa (Snowdon) via the Pyg / Miners' Tracks**
Start / Finish LL55 4NU or SH 647 556 or ///fast.jeeps.splashes

Route 9   **Ben Nevis, Scottish Highlands**
Start / Finish PH33 6SX or NN 123 730 or ///reduce.incurring.verges

Route 10   **Cadair Idris, Eryri (Snowdonia) National Park**
Start / Finish LL36 9AJ or SH 732 115 or ///warmers.lighters.reports

Route 11   **Scafell Pike, Lake District National Park**
Start / Finish CA20 1EX or NY 187 085 or ///currently.switched.tile

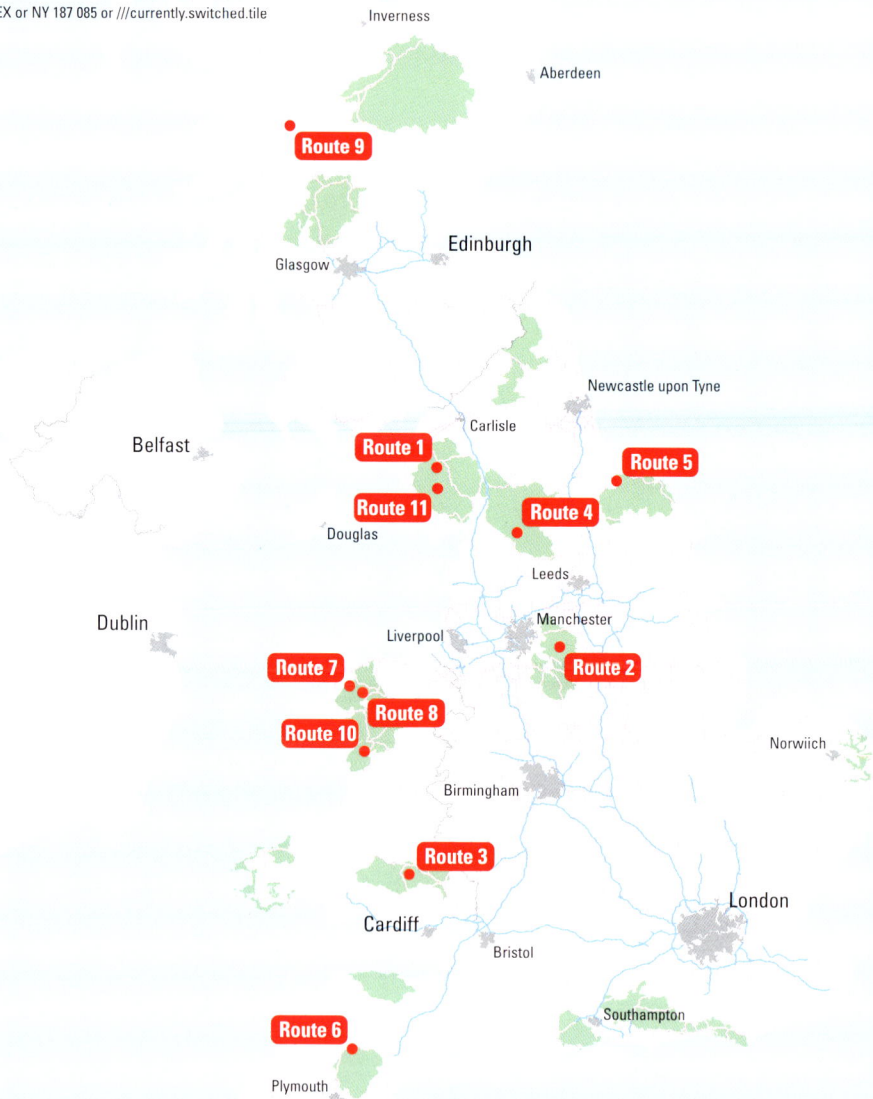

Inverness

Aberdeen

Route 9

Edinburgh

Glasgow

Newcastle upon Tyne

Belfast

Carlisle

Route 1

Route 5

Route 11

Route 4

Douglas

Leeds

Dublin

Manchester

Liverpool

Route 2

Norwiich

Route 7

Route 8

Route 10

Birmingham

London

Route 3

Cardiff

Bristol

Southampton

Route 6

Plymouth

The views, even from this small mountain, are breathtaking.

Cat Bells, Lake District

Height	451m (1,480ft)
Total height gain	462m (1,516ft)
Distance	5.95km (3.7 miles)
Total time	2-3 hours
Grade	EASY
Start / Finish	CA12 5UE or NY 246 211 or ///noisy.curtains.tutorial

Cat Bells, while smaller than many of its Lake District neighbours, is a great 'starter hill' for those looking for their first mountain climbing experience. Situated just a few miles from Keswick and easily accessible, this short walk will give you immense satisfaction as well as spectacular views and a real sense of what it's like to be in the mountains.

Our route starts from Hawse End on the west bank of Derwentwater. There's really nothing else here, so be sure to bring everything with you. There's a very small car park on the Skelgill road and some roadside parking if you're lucky. An even better option is to leave your car in nearby Keswick and take the boat across Derwentwater. There are regular shuttles during the summer between Keswick and Hawse End, as well as circular trips around the lake that stop at various landing stages. Ask locally or search online for 'Hawse End shuttle service' for more information.

If arriving by boat, you'll need to walk up through the woods, past the Hawse End Outdoor Centre, turn left at the main road and you'll arrive at the car park and our starting point.

START From the car park follow the signpost signed 'Cat Bells 1 mile'. This is a clear, easy-to-follow path that zigzags up and onto the ridge, directly to the summit. There are a couple of steeper sections where you might need to use your hands for support, but certainly nothing close to scrambling. Look around you as you're climbing – the views of Derwentwater to your left and the fells in all directions are truly spectacular. It's quite steep at times, with a brief respite around halfway followed by an even steeper climb to the top, so if you're not used to mountain walking, take it easy.

As you get close to the summit there are numerous path options but, as long as you're heading uphill, you're heading in the right direction.

It shouldn't take you long to reach the summit and when you get there it's like standing on top of a rock. Hopefully you're there on a beautiful summer's day and can really take in the views. Grab a drink and a snack and be happy that it's downhill for the rest of the walk.

❶ When you're ready, continue in the same direction, on a much more gradual descent until you reach a little dip. ❷ Take the path to your left that heads steeply downhill. This stone path zigzags its way down, before straightening out to skirt around the hill.

❸ Towards the bottom of the hill, just above the treeline, a path heads off to your left. If you're just here to bag the peak and not interested in anything else, you can take this path directly back to the start point. However, hopefully you're looking for a bit more of a walk, so instead carry on ahead. Pass through a gate and follow the path around to the right which takes you down to the road. Turn right here, walking along the road, past the houses and look out for a gate on your left, signposted 'Lodor – 1 mile'. ❹ This is the Cumbria Way National Trail and will lead you gently down to the banks of Derwentwater.

Cross over the stream, using the small bridge if you need to. The easy-to-follow path passes through farmland and adjacent to a wooded area. Go through a kissing gate and when you reach the next gate, take the path option to your left. Walk over the duckboards then bear right, walking down to the shore. As you get close to the lake look up to your left and you'll have a great view of where you've walked so far.

❺ You're now at the south end of Derwentwater, with Keswick being at the far north end. The path runs alongside the

The start of your walk is clearly signposted from the small car park.

left bank, all the way back to your start point and is easy to follow. This is a beautiful section to walk along as it mixes the waterside with forests and open land, and there are plenty of opportunities to sit and relax on the water's edge, or even take a swim - with fantastic views back up to Cat Bells throughout.

The path skirts around a lovely lakeside house where you'll need to climb a short, unpaved stretch before turning right through a gate. (6) Where the path splits in two, stick with the right-hand option nearest the water. Here there is a landing stage and, if the boats are operating, there's an opportunity to catch a ferry back to Keswick, with a circular tour of the lake.

7 At the next landing stage, pass through the gate and turn left. You'll have more great views of Cat Bells and the entire ridge you walked along earlier, up to your left. Head through a gate and follow the path around to your right, which leads you into the grounds of the Hawse End Outdoor Centre. If you travelled over from Keswick on the ferry, you could bear right here for a short cut down to the jetty, otherwise carry on straight. When you reach the tarmac track, turn right and follow it up to the road. Turn left around the outdoor centre car park and then right along a footpath through the trees, which will take you back to where you started.

The popular Mam Tor ridge   *Photo: Cpsl42, Dreamstime.com*

Mam Tor, Peak District, Derbyshire

Height	517m (1,696ft)
Total height gain	489m (1,604ft)
Distance	12.5km (7.75 miles)
Total time	3-4 hours
Grade	EASY
Start / Finish	S33 8WH or SK 149 830 or ///hydration.best.gender

At 517m at its highest point, we're going to struggle to call Mam Tor a mountain by any definition, but I've decided to include it as it's a great 'starter' hill and has always been one of my favourites. Unfortunately, it's a lot of other people's favourite too, so definitely one to avoid on a bank holiday weekend. You'll find Mam Tor in the heart of the Peak District, making it easily accessible from Manchester and Sheffield.

The walk starts from Castleton, a lovely Peak District village, popular with tourists due to its location and number of pubs and tea shops, all of which I'd highly recommend exploring after your walk. Right in the centre of the village is a large car

159

and coach park with a visitor centre and public toilets. There is parking for over 130 cars, although in the height of summer this will fill up quickly. More roadside parking is available a few minutes away, on the road up to Winnats Pass.

Public transport is a bit sketchy around this part of the Peak District. Buses do operate in and out of Castleton, but you'll need to check local timetables for up-to-date service information. Trains stop at Hope, which is the next village just a mile or so away on the Manchester to Sheffield line. A short walk from the station into Hope village will let you pick up the walk from there.

START Take the opportunity before leaving the car park to use the facilities as there are no more until you get back in a few hours' time. As you exit, look behind you and, in the distance, you will see the aptly named Great Ridge, along which you'll be walking a bit later.

Turn left out of the car park and walk along the pavements through the village. You'll pass a few local shops where you can pick up any last-minute supplies. Make a mental note of which pub you fancy for your post-walk pint! The road bends sharply left and then right. Stick to the pavement as you make your way out of the village. The road will be busy in the summer so take care crossing, although traffic will usually be moving slowly due to the sharp bends.

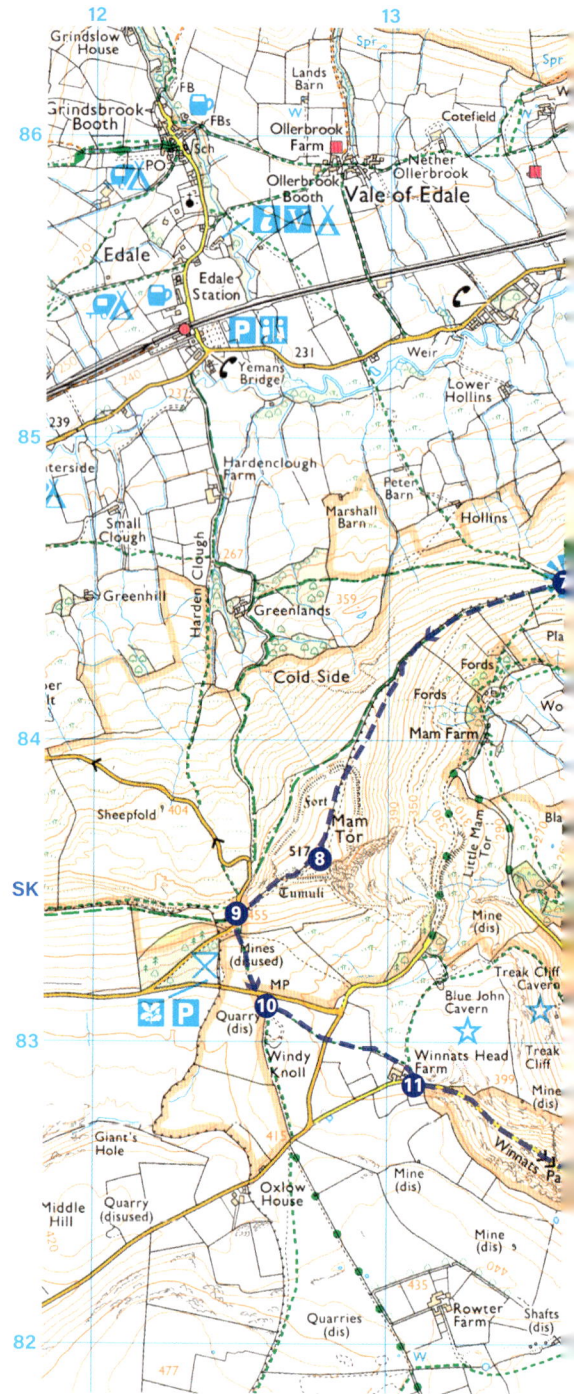

❶ Continue past a small road junction on your right and, before the road bends to the left, look out for a footpath heading right, beside a stone wall in the corner of a small field. The path is signposted 'PUBLIC FOOTPATH TO HOPE'. Follow this, which quickly turns into a track running behind some houses.

Eventually, you'll find yourself out in fields, but the track is well worn and easy to follow. After about 1,300m (around 15 minutes walking) you'll reach the railway line, which is used by the nearby cement works. Cross carefully, taking note of the instructions on the sign, and continue along the path for a short distance until it comes out onto a road. ❷ Turn left and follow this into the village of Hope. ❸ When you reach the main road with the pub on your left and shops in front of you, cross over and turn left – walking for about 50m, keeping an eye out for a public footpath on your right in between two houses. Take this, and after a short distance the path emerges onto a small housing estate. Go right when you reach the road, and at the next road, cross over and head through the gate to the left of the primary school.

❹ The path now takes you out of the village, into the countryside and up onto the Great Ridge at Lose Hill (pronounced 'Loose' Hill). It's very popular and easy to follow but does become quite steep later on, so pace yourself. You'll walk along the edge of a few fields and cross back over the railway line, but this time using a rickety footbridge. Then it's on through farmyards and out into farmers' fields, always heading in the same direction. Lose Hill will quickly become visible in the distance. It's going to get steeper and steeper, and when another path joins you from the right you know you're on the final stretch. ❺ A bit further on the path splits; continue straight on, steeply uphill along the nicely laid stone path until you reach the summit stone at the top of Lose Hill. ❻ This viewpoint is a lovely spot for a drink and a snack, knowing that you've got the toughest of the day's climbing out of the way. There are a few rocky outcrops here which can provide great shelter from any wind. Behind, you'll see the villages of Hope and Castleton, in front of you is the Kinder plateau and to your left is Mam Tor. On a nice day the views here are stunning.

When you're ready, continue on the path heading along the ridge, with the next peak of Hollins Cross in the distance. Route finding from now until you reach Mam Tor is pretty simple – just keep walking along the ridge and you can't go far wrong. You're high up here, but the path is good so there's nothing to fear. You'll reach Back Tor first, with its steep 'staircase' down to Hollins Cross. To your right you should be able to see down to the village of Edale, on the other side of the Manchester to Sheffield railway line, and on the other side of the valley is Kinder, where you will find Kinder Scout and the Kinder plateau, the highest point in the Peak District (and notoriously difficult to find).

The view looking along the Great Ridge from Lose Hill, with Mam Tor in the distance.

7 The summit stone at Hollins Cross is so named as several footpaths converge here. This is another impressive viewpoint. To your right the path leads to Edale, and to your left back to Castleton. If you're starting to get tired and don't think you can do much more, the path on your left is your escape route back to the start point.

Carry straight on as your target should be very visible now. The path up to Mam Tor starts to steepen but it's a nice, gradual uphill walk so keep at it, and you'll be there in no time.

8 The summit of Mam Tor is marked with a trig point – a large stone pillar originally used for surveying. It's tradition when climbing a hill or mountain to touch the trig point; it's less traditional, but still great fun, to climb and stand aloft it! (Warning: I suppose I should say don't do this unless you're pretty nimble, as a fall can really hurt.)

This is the highest point of your walk and if it's a nice day the views will be amazing. I should also point out that I've experienced one of my windiest ever days on Mam Tor, which saw me on my hands and knees, crawling around the summit desperately clinging on for dear life. That really was an awesome day.

Unsurprisingly, it's downhill all the way now, but it's no less interesting with one of the Peak District's most outstanding geological features still to come. When you're ready, continue in the same direction, descending steeply down a beautifully laid stone staircase until you reach the road. ❾ Go through the gate and turn left, continuing down more steps and straight across the field in the same direction. You're heading for a gap in the wall in the distance. Cross carefully over the busy road and through another gate, but quickly look for a faint path bearing left rather than the obvious path going straight on. ❿ The path left will lead you to another hole in a wall where you again cross a road and continue on behind a farm, before coming out onto Winnats Pass. ⓫ Turn left and walk carefully along the road down into the gorge. You will have traffic joining you but it's a narrow road and it will usually be moving slowly. Further down, there are grass verges so you'll be able to get off the tarmac.

Winnats Pass is a limestone valley that was under the sea 350 million years ago. What you see today was created by melting glaciers wearing away the rock and gradually dissolving it. Streams formed and flowed through and under cracks in the rock, creating a large underground cave system, which eventually collapsed leaving a steep-sided valley. The area is now a Site of Special Scientific Interest (SSSI).

Follow the road down to the bottom of the pass where you'll reach a gate leading into the car park for Speedwell Cavern, which offers underground boat trips through the extensive cave network – a

My niece and nephew standing aloft the trig point on top of Mam Tor. They were definitely OK with this and weren't nervous at all!

highly recommended activity for another day. Continue along the pavement, turning right at the road junction then on into the village. When you reach the mini roundabout, the car park you started from is to your left.

Well done! Wash your boots off in the stream and go find one of those nice pubs in the village.

The magnificent Pen y Fan, Bannau Brycheiniog (Brecon Beacons)

Route 3

Pen y Fan, South Wales

Height	886m (2,907ft)
Total height gain	542m (1,778ft)
Distance	7.6km (4.75 miles)
Total time	2.5-3 hours
Grade	EASY
Start / Finish	LD3 8NL or SN 983 203 or ///encourage.extreme.autumn

Pen y Fan, in the heart of the Bannau Brycheiniog / Brecon Beacons National Park, holds the accolade of being the highest mountain in South Wales. At an impressive 886m (2,907ft), you might think it beyond a beginner walk, but in fact it's a fairly easy summit to reach. This is helped hugely by the fact that my walk starts at 440m, so you're already halfway there before you get out of the car. The mountain is owned and managed by the National Trust and is frequently used by the military, so don't be surprised / scared if you come across soldiers with huge rucksacks, making light work of the climb.

The walk starts from the Storey Arms on the A470, between Brecon and Merthyr Tydfil, and part of its attraction is its

165

proximity to these towns. There is limited parking available in a large layby opposite the Storey Arms, and further parking in laybys 500m along the road in each direction. The Pont ar Daf car park, south of the Storey Arms, is on the walk route so is particularly useful. All these fill up quickly on busy summer weekends. Depending on the time of the year, each of the three laybys usually has a refreshment van of some sort, particularly at weekends and during holidays.

A regular bus service operates up to seven times a day between Cardiff and Brecon and beyond, stopping at the Storey Arms. This provides easy access to walkers coming from as far away as Merthyr Tydfil, Pontypridd, Builth Wells and Newtown.

START Once you've got over the disappointment that the Storey Arms isn't a pub but is actually Cardiff City Council's outdoor education centre, look for the footpath on the left of the buildings by a red telephone box. This is the start of the walk. Head through the kissing gate and follow the well-laid stone path uphill. It's easy to follow (if you're using an Ordnance Survey map, you're going to follow the black dashed 'path' as opposed to the green dashed 'right of way' – you should already understand the differences after reading the navigation chapter). The incline soon flattens out, just in time for you to drop down into a small valley to cross over a stream. ❶ The path continues relatively straight, with the impressive peak of Corn Du ahead of you in the

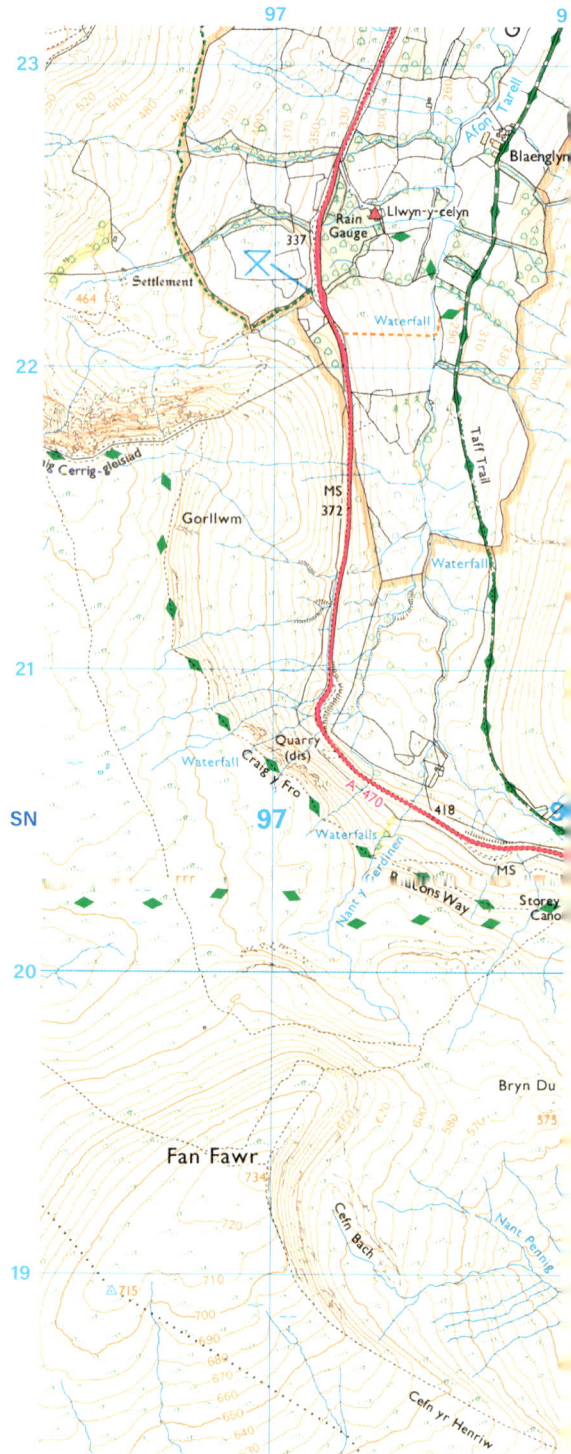

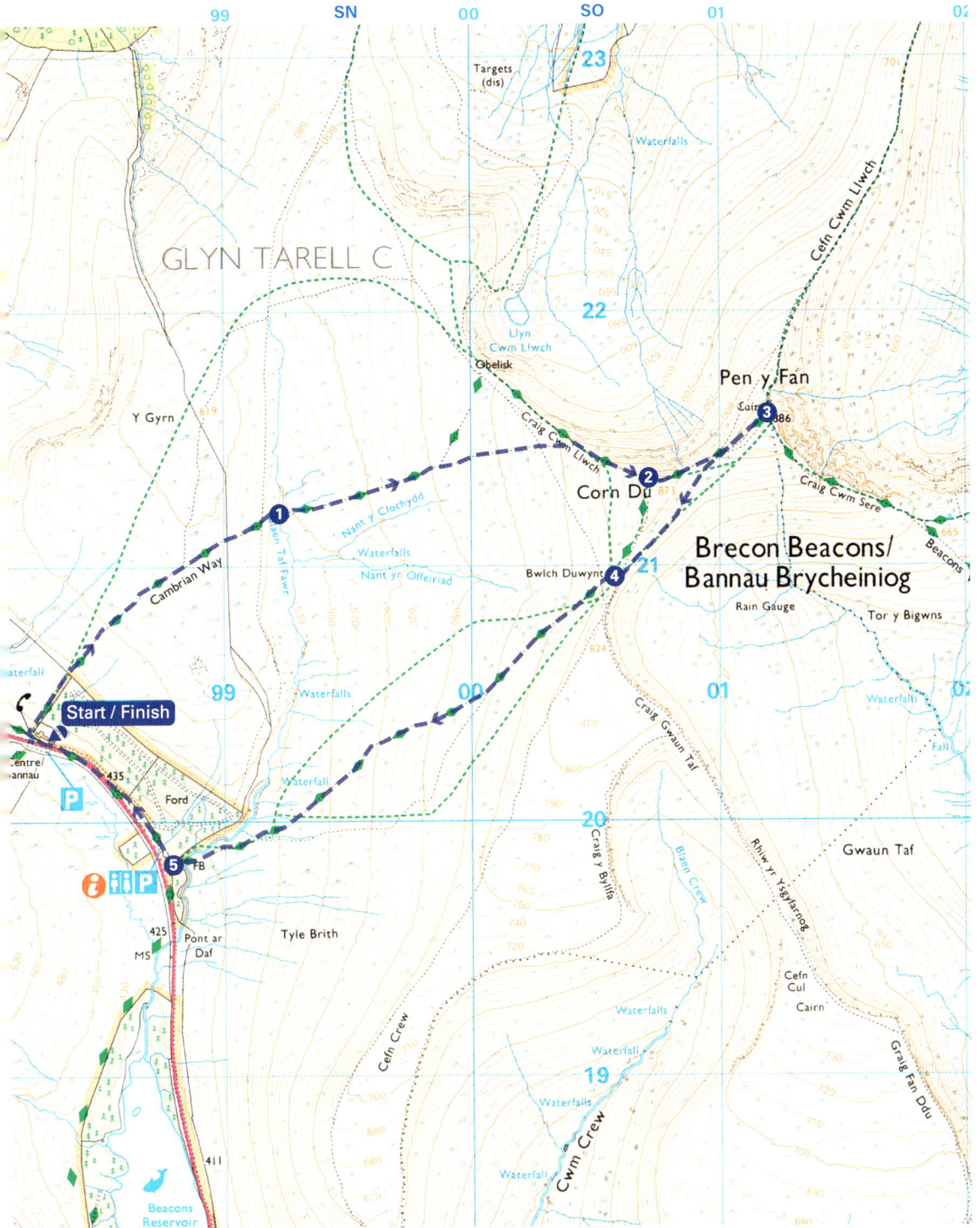

The unmistakeable top of Pen y Fan

distance. Don't worry, it looks worse than it is. Carry on along the path as it alternates between easy-to-walk-on gravel and larger stones. The incline is steady, right up until the foot of Corn Du where it's gets pretty steep. This is only a few minutes' hard work, and once you get to the top you can be happy knowing that the worst of the climbing for the day is over. Clamber over the rocks at the top of the path, onto the small plateau with a Bronze Age cairn (a pile of stones which was once a burial chamber). ❷ This is Corn Du, the second highest point in South Wales at 873m (2,864ft) and a good chance for a drink and a snack.

Look over to your left and you'll see the summit of Pen y Fan, almost within touching distance. The path continues to your left and it's a relatively easy wander to the top. ❸ The summit area is quite large with another Bronze Age burial chamber marking the highest point. There are very steep drops just beyond the cairn, so if you're walking with kids be sure to keep them close by. The views here are spectacular with mountains in all directions.

When you're ready to set off again, retrace your steps back to Corn Du. Ignore the climb back up to it and instead, just carry on along the flat path bearing left. After around 750m you'll reach a cairn marking Bwlch Duwynt. ❹ Turn to the right here and follow the well laid path downhill in the same direction, all the way to the main road. You'll arrive at the Pont ar Daf car park further along the road. ❺ Turn right to walk through the car park then along the footpath which runs adjacent to the road, back to the Storey Arms.

The path leading up to the summit of Pen-y-ghent.

Route 4

Pen-y-ghent, Yorkshire Dales

Height	694m (2,277ft)
Total height gain	470m (1,542ft)
Distance	9.7km (6 miles)
Total time	3 hours
Grade	EASY
Start / Finish	BD24 0HF or SD 808 726 or ///covertly.overture.cloak

Although the smallest of the Yorkshire Three Peaks, Pen-y-ghent is perhaps the most stunning. Its imposing stature stands out right from the start.

The walk starts from the small Yorkshire village of Horton in Ribblesdale. It's hugely popular with walkers and extremely busy on summer weekends, as it's also the traditional start of the Yorkshire Three Peaks Challenge. This involves people climbing Pen-y-ghent then going on to tackle nearby Whernside and Ingleborough, all in under 12 hours (read more in Chapter 19).

There's a small public car park in the centre of the village but on weekends it will fill up quickly. If there's no room here, head north out of the village, following the road round to the left and a few hundred metres after the two bridges you'll come across a farmer who regularly opens his field for extra parking. You might be lucky and find some on-road parking on the edge of the village, but please avoid parking in front of resident's houses.

There are also excellent public transport options available. Buses pass through the village from nearby Settle, and trains on the Leeds to Carlisle line stop at the train station just on the edge of the village.

Horton has a couple of pubs, a café and tea room, all of which would welcome your business after your walk. I can also highly recommend one of the fabulous fish and chip shops in nearby Settle if you're looking for treat food on your way home.

🏃 **START** From the village car park, turn right and head along the Settle road. You'll pass a red phone box and the Trading Post village shop. After around 500m, the road bends to the left around St Oswald's Church. ❶ After the church, take the second road on the left immediately after the bridge and head out of the village, past some lovely old stone houses and the local school, and into the trees. Stay on this road as it continues alongside the stream, until you come to some farm buildings then take the footpath on your left through two sets of gates.

❷ Turn left and follow the wall steeply uphill. The path soon opens out and you'll be met with a fantastic view of Pen-y-ghent

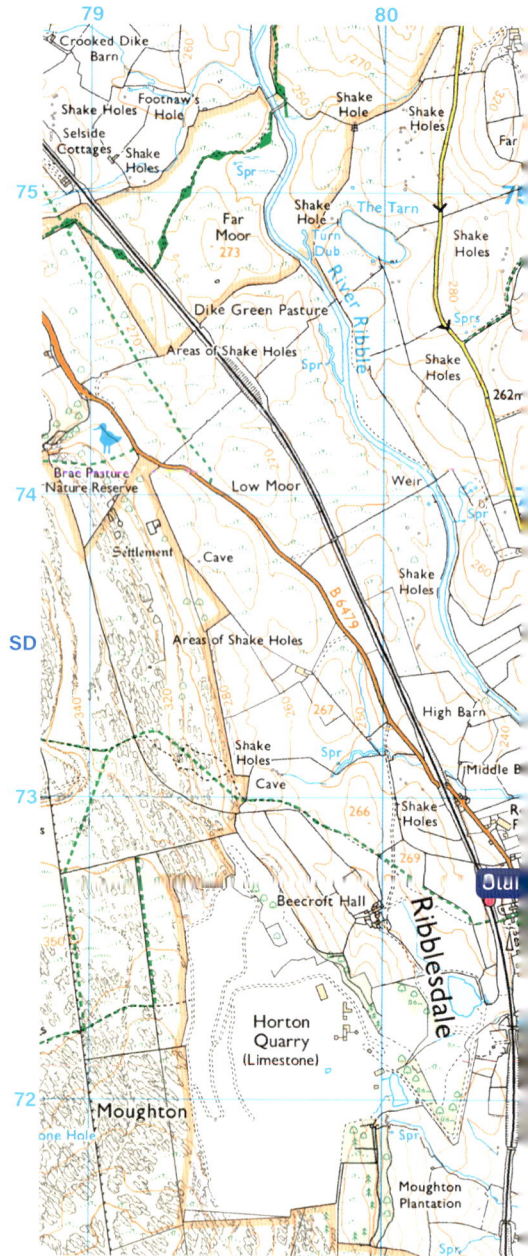

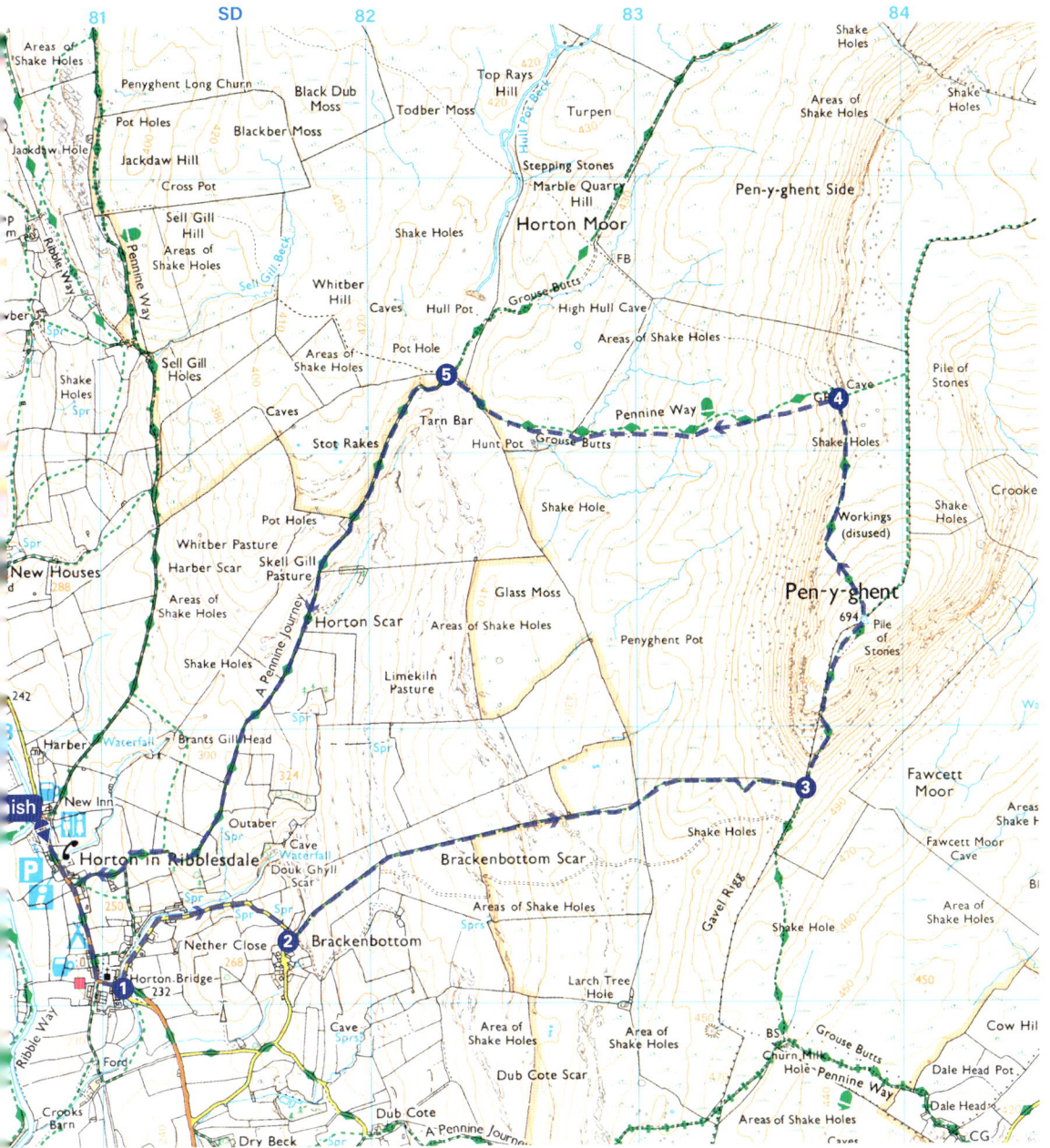

Walkers approaching the summit.
Photo: Rambling Tog, Dreamstime.com

There's not a huge amount on top of Pen-y-ghent other than a couple of quirky shelters built into the stone wall, but the views are amazing.

When you've caught your breath and grabbed a snack, pass through either hole in the wall and continue along the Pennine Way, heading gently downhill. It soon turns into a staircase made of large steps. ❹ The path will eventually turn 90° to the left and descend steeply back towards to the village. There's been a lot of path restoration work in this area in recent years (due to the ever-increasing popularity of the Yorkshire Three Peaks Challenge), so please avoid 'cutting corners' and keep to the path.

❺ At the next junction, turn left (signposted 'Pennine Way - Horton in Ribblesdale'). At this point you're likely to see lots of people continuing straight on as they head towards Whernside, the second of the Yorkshire Three Peaks. Ignore everyone else and keep to the path downhill to the left.

Follow the Pennine Way all the way back to Horton in Ribblesdale alongside farmers' fields, and eventually residential dwellings. Continue back into the village until you pop out onto the main road. Turn right here for the short walk back to the car park.

ahead. The route here is easy to follow. The path levels out and steepens a few times as you cross into Open Access land and approach the mountain from its right. ❸ Eventually, you'll come to a T-junction in the path where you'll need to turn left for the final 700m climb to the summit. You're now walking along the Pennine Way, England's first National Trail and one of the UK's most famous long-distance walks, stretching for 268 miles from the Peak District to the Scottish border.

The path bends around to the right and climbs up a beautiful 'natural' staircase fashioned out of the rock. It does get a bit 'scrambly' here, but it's simple enough and nothing that should cause any concern. The ground flattens out a bit as you follow the stone cairns upwards.

Roseberry Topping looking magnificent in the distance.

Roseberry Topping, North Yorkshire

Height	320m (1,050ft)
Total height gain	214m (702ft)
Distance	3.2km (2 miles)
Total time	1 hour
Grade	EASY
Start / Finish	TS9 6QS or NZ 570 128 or ///trimmer.configure.expand

Although a long way from being an actual mountain, Roseberry Topping is a great 'training hill' for those in the North East of England. Its unique shape is visible for miles around, and its distinctive look often leads to comparisons with the famous Matterhorn in the Swiss Alps.

This is a really easy walk, suitable for absolute beginners and will be a big hit with young children. Although there's a short steep section to contend with, the reward is worth it. It's a great opportunity to test your legs as the incline is similar to what you'd expect on a bigger mountain – there's just much less of it here.

Roseberry Topping is managed by the National Trust, and you'll find a small public car park with seasonal toilet facilities on the A173. There's little else around here so be sure to bring everything you need with

173

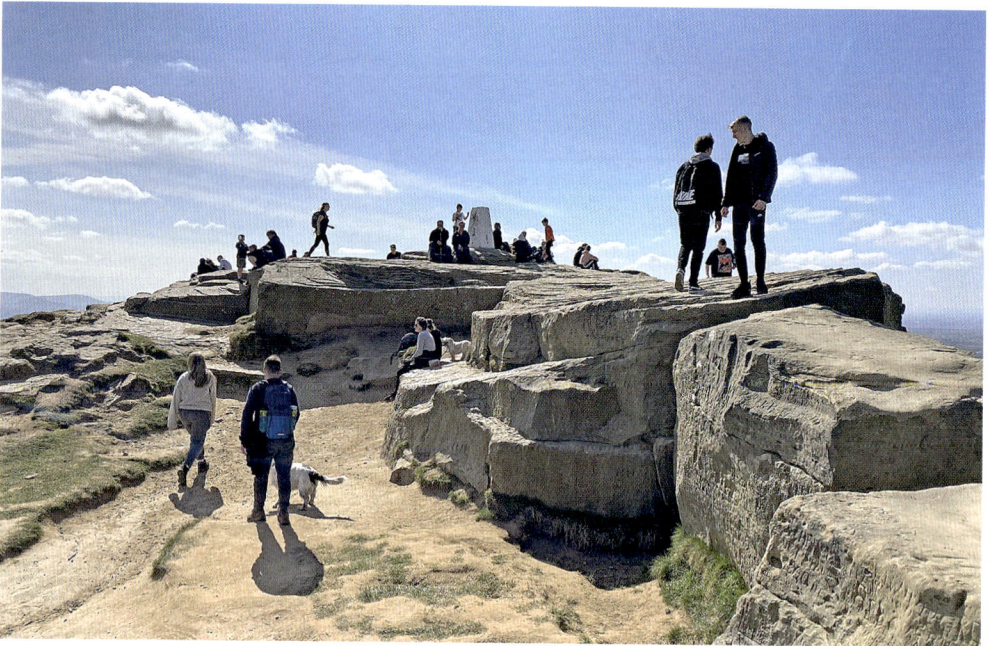

Exploring the summit of Roseberry Topping.

you. On summer weekends you have the bonus of an ice cream van. Unfortunately, there aren't any great public transport options. A bus from Middlesbrough to Guisborough and Stokesley will get you fairly close. Check local timetables for up-to-date info.

START Follow the path out the back of the car park and turn right along Roseberry Lane. Pass through the gate and straight away you will have an amazing view of the challenge ahead.

The woodland in front of you is Newton Wood, which you'll need to pass through to reach Roseberry Topping. ❶ Go up the steps at the entrance to the woods, pass through the gate and head straight up more steps in front of you. These lead to

a small clearing with a bench and straight into yet another steep set of steps!

❷ When you get to the top of the steps, the path turns right for a final set of steps, this time made out of stone. Take your time as you tackle these climbs. Look down to your right and you'll already see how much height you've gained in just a short time.

❸ The path turns left through a gate and up more steps with Roseberry Topping dead ahead.

Make your way steeply up to the summit, taking your time until you reach the white trig point sat proudly on the rocky top. Enjoy the views, grab a drink, then, when you're ready, descend along the stone

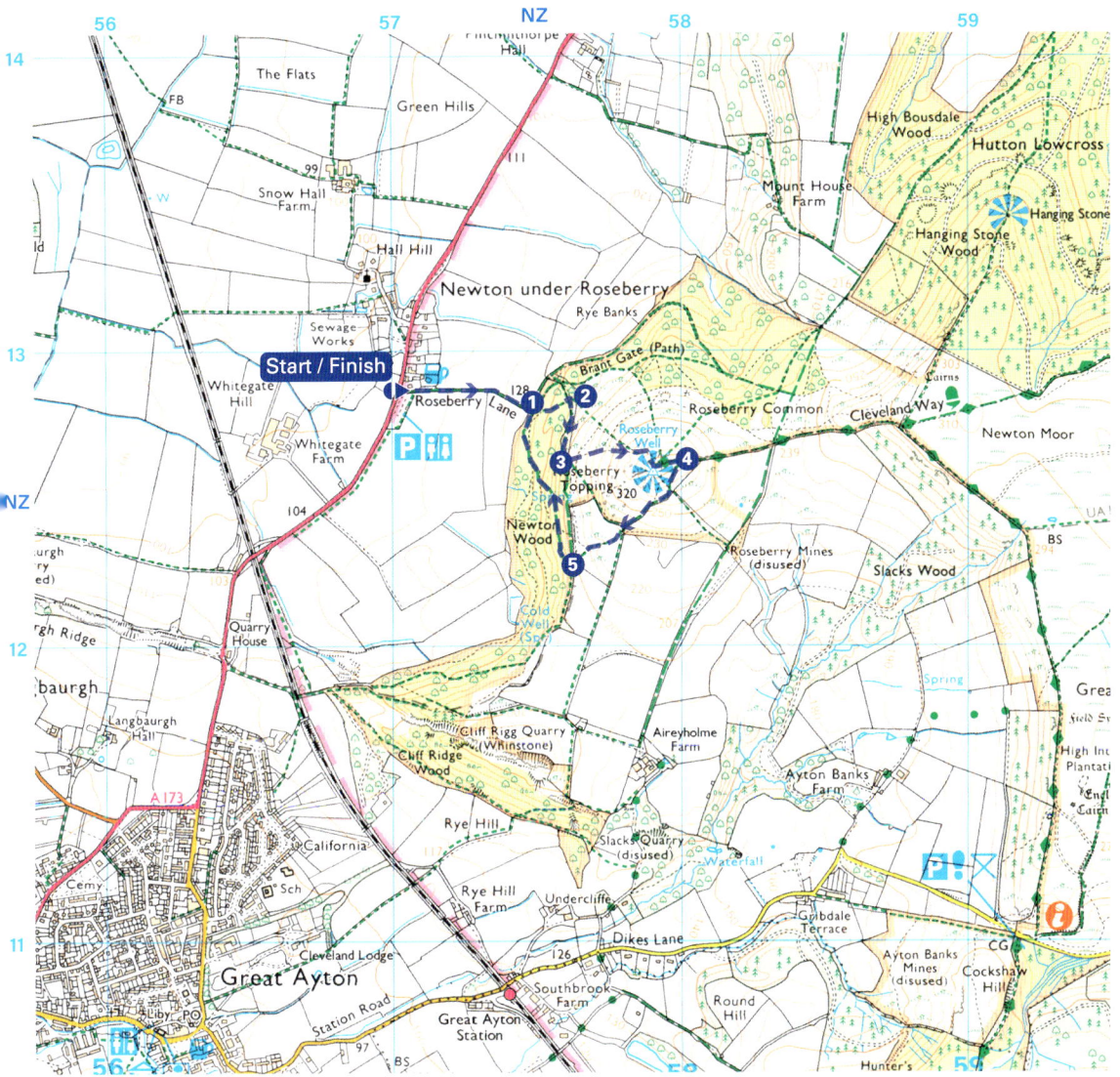

The final push to the summit. Please keep to the stone path here to help reduce erosion.

path on the opposite side of the hill to where you came up. ❹ When you reach the fence, turn right (don't go through the gate). Try and stick to the stepped paths going down rather than attempting a shortcut down the grass slopes.

Look back for a different, but equally impressive, view of Roseberry Topping's sharp face. Follow the fence line across the grass in the direction of an old shooting hut and then turn right, back down into Newton Wood. ❺ At the entrance to the wood, go through the gate and, ignoring the yellow arrow pointing left, go straight on steeply down into the woods.

Continue through the woods and, as the descent becomes easier, you'll find yourself back at the gate leading to Roseberry Lane. Follow the lane down to the main road and turn left back into the car park.

Yes Tor with High Willhays showing in the distance.   Photo: Max Piper

Route 6

Yes Tor and High Willhays, Dartmoor

Height	621m (2,039ft)
Total height gain	421m (1,381ft)
Distance	9.7km (6 miles)
Total time	3-4 hours
Grade	MODERATE
Start / Finish	EX20 4LU or SX 561 918 or ///cross.sung.printout

Dartmoor National Park, in the South West of England, is made up of vast moorland and isn't typically known for its mountains. However, there are features you can climb and if you're based in this part of the country, they make great starter hills until you're able to venture further north.

I've rated this walk as MODERATE, not because it's particularly challenging (in fact it's a very easy ascent), but because navigation can be tricky. In many places you'll find yourself walking across open moorland and paths might be vague or even non-existent at times. This is very typical of Dartmoor, and for these reasons this walk should only be attempted on a clear day with good weather. Getting lost on the moor is a very real possibility.

You should also be (very!) aware that both Yes Tor and High Willhays are inside the Okehampton Firing Range used by the MOD. Look out for red flags during the daytime and red lamps at night – these indicate that live firing is taking place within the range, which is marked by red and white poles. Even better, check in advance by searching online for 'Dartmoor firing times'. The MOD do a great job of tidying up after themselves, but it goes without saying that you shouldn't touch any military debris you might stumble upon.

The walk starts from Meldon Reservoir, near Meldon village and just a few minutes off the A30 Okehampton Bypass. There's a good-sized car park but sadly little or no public transport in this area.

START Turn left out of the car park, pass through the gate and walk along the track towards Meldon Reservoir. Cross over the dam then turn right, keeping the reservoir on your right. ❶ After around 250m, at a junction, the path will turn back on itself almost 180° as it starts to climb away from the water, up Longstone Hill. Although on an Ordnance Survey map this is shown as a track, there's nothing really on the ground here except a worn path in the grass.

The path bends round to the right and then to the left again and eventually becomes more and more vague. This is where you

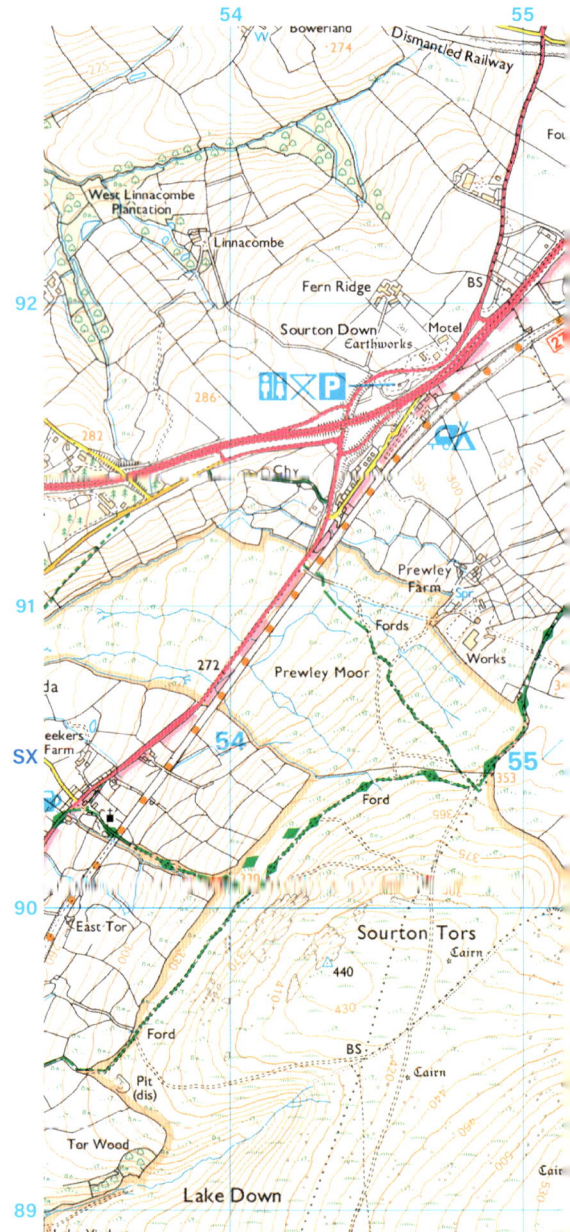

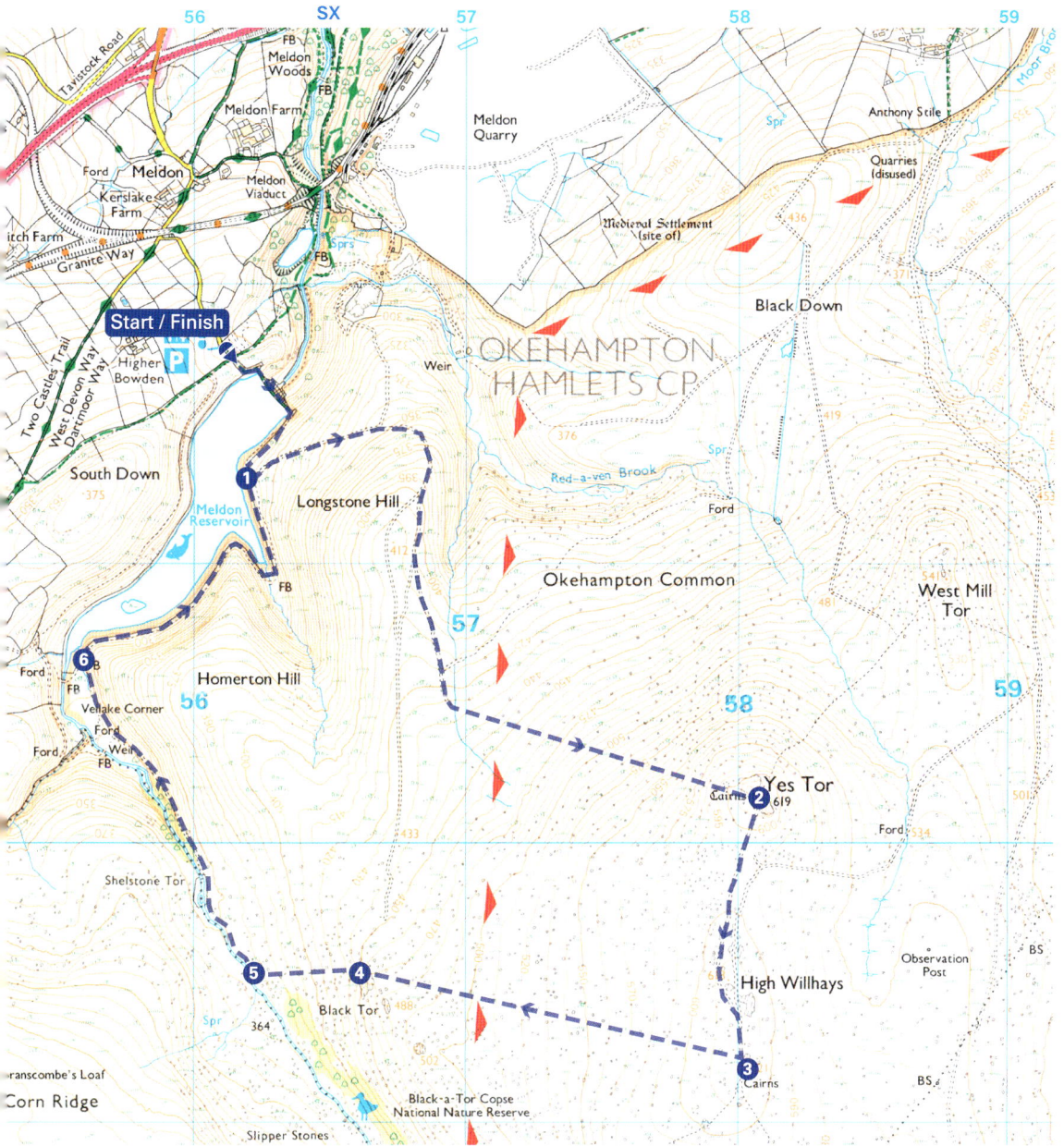

Map created by Lovell Johns Limited. Based upon Ordnance Survey digital map data
© Crown Copyright 2023 Licence Number 43368U. All rights reserved.

The cairn atop High Willhays *Photo: Max Piper*

need to start looking into the distance to find what you're aiming for. Yes Tor is the second highest point on Dartmoor and has a trig point on top, so on a clear day (and you should only be attempting this walk on such a day) you should be able to spot it ahead. Just keep heading uphill the most direct way you can.

② Your next peak is High Willhays and is just under 1km almost directly south from your current position. There is a vague path to follow but you're looking for the next highest point on Dartmoor, marked by a large pile of stones, so keep your eyes peeled.

③ The descent from here back to the reservoir needs some concentration, as there are even fewer obvious paths to follow. With Yes Tor behind you, you're

looking for a small, rocky outcrop directly to your right around 1.3km away. This is Black Tor and what you want to aim for. It's the most obvious way down the hill and is a fairly steady descent. **④** Once you reach Black Tor, bear left slightly down towards the West Okement River. **⑤** Keeping the river on your left, follow it back down towards the reservoir and eventually a path becomes more obvious

⑥ Once you reach the reservoir, turn right keeping the water on your left. There's a small dog-leg where you'll cross a footbridge, and then simply follow the path back to the dam and the car park.

The magnificent summit of Yr Wyddfa (Snowdon), seen from the Miners' Track.

Yr Wyddfa (Snowdon), Eryri (Snowdonia), North Wales

Snowdon or Yr Wyddfa (pronounced 'err with va'), as it's known in Welsh, is one of our most popular mountains. It has the honour of being the highest mountain in Wales and is, in fact, the highest peak in the UK outside of the Scottish Highlands. While it might be 260m shorter than its 'Three Peaks' rival Ben Nevis, it benefits from being considerably more accessible. It's only a five-hour drive from London, three hours from Birmingham and around two hours from Manchester or Liverpool (driving times from London to Ben Nevis are closer to ten hours!)

There are drawbacks to this convenience. You may have seen news stories of parking problems and queues on the summit as walkers wait patiently for their photo opportunity. However, the days on which you'll experience this aren't that frequent and, if you absolutely must tackle the mountain on a summer bank holiday weekend, there are still ways you can beat the crowds (see Chapter 5, When to Go).

There are six main routes to the summit, leading up all sides of the mountain. The two 'easiest' and most popular are the Llanberis Path, named after the village of Llanberis where the path starts from, and the Pyg / Miners' Tracks, which both start from the

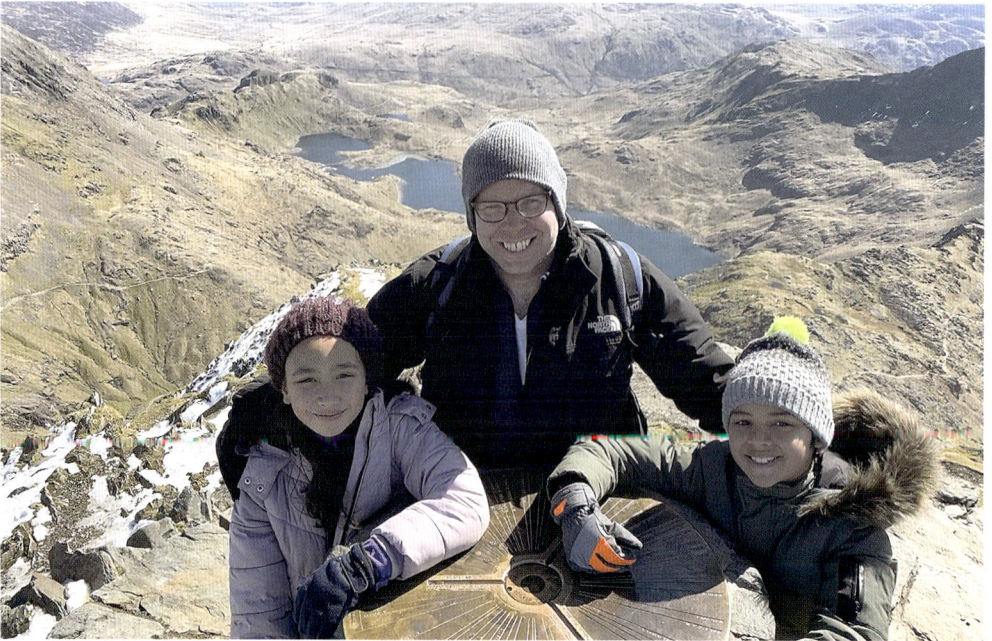

Enjoy your summit selfie. What you can see around you will depend entirely on the weather.

top of Pen y Pass, about five miles from Llanberis. Which you choose will depend on a few factors.

The Llanberis Path is widely regarded as the 'easiest' way up, and in normal summer conditions it's little more than a long, uphill walk with a couple of short but very steep sections. However, it's around 14.5km (nine miles) there and back, so it's also the longest route.

The Pyg Track, conversely, is the shortest and starts around 150m higher up the mountain. Coupled with the Miners' Track, this makes a nice circular walk, however there are a few sections where you'll need to work hard and use your hands for support.

There are a number of public transport options around the area. It's quite feasible to get a fast(ish) train from London to Bangor, then a local bus to Llanberis or Pen y Pass. Llanberis also has several shops and dining options, as well as a wide variety of accommodation for those staying over.

Waving at the train from the Llanberis Path.

Route 7

Yr Wyddfa (Snowdon) via the Llanberis Path

Height	1085m (3,560ft)
Total height gain	984m (3,228ft)
Distance	14.4km (9 miles)
Total time	6-7 hours
Grade	MODERATE
Start / Finish	LL55 4TU or SH 583 598 or ///shady.ground.joys

There's plenty of (rarely good value) parking available in Llanberis. The largest, most convenient, and therefore most expensive, can be found directly opposite the Snowdon Mountain Railway Station. You'll save a few pounds using smaller car parks further into the village, but having your car waiting nearby when you finish your walk is usually worth the extra. You will make yourself very unpopular with the locals and probably receive a parking ticket if you try and park in side streets or in resident permit areas, so please stick to the main car parks in the village.

Make your way to the far west of the village, where you'll find the Snowdon Mountain Railway Station. Here you can

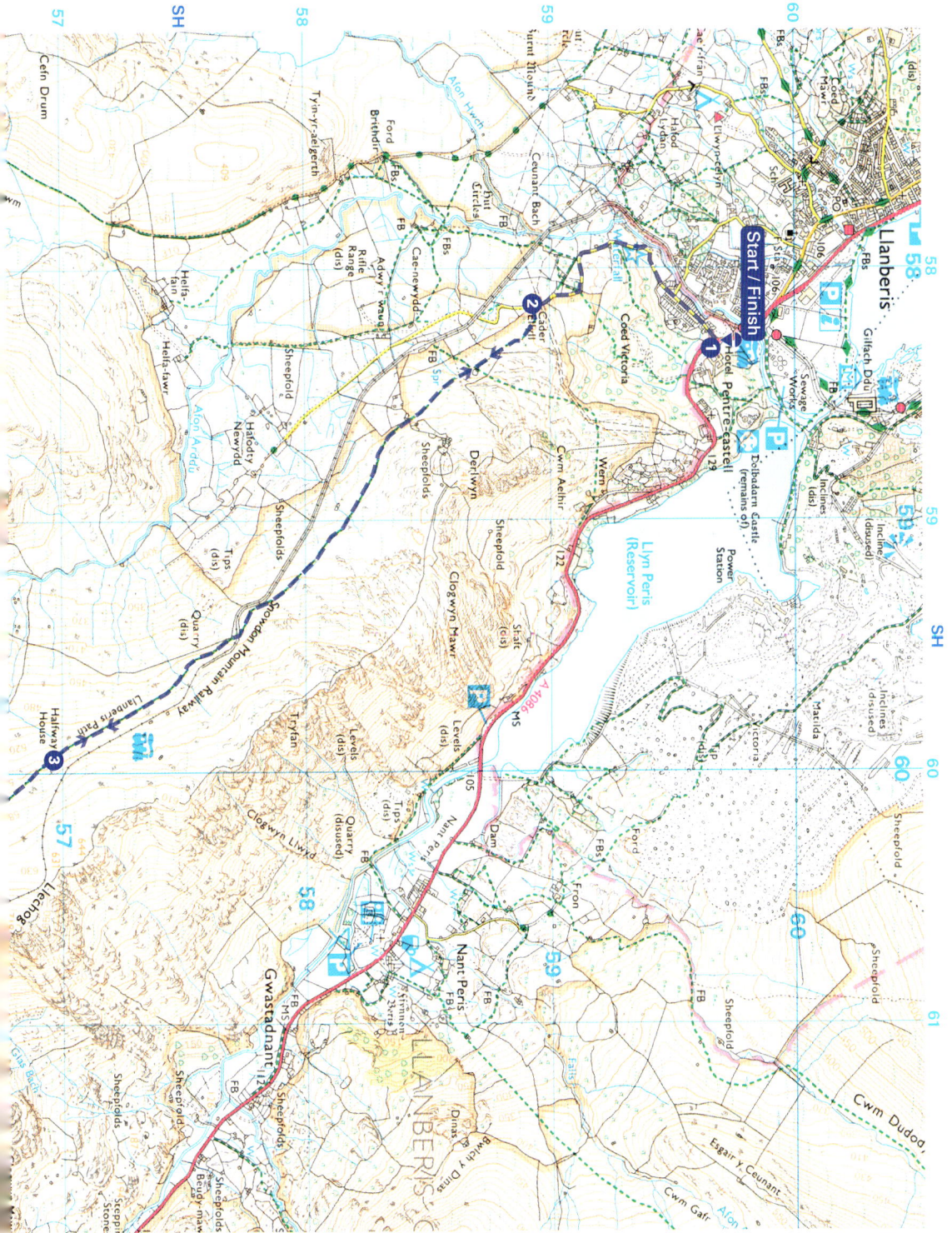

Be sure to turn around and look at the height you've gained already.

grin at the tourists taking the hour-long, uncomfortable train ride to the summit, knowing you'll have a much greater sense of achievement at the end of the day.

🏃 **START** With your back to the railway station, turn right and walk away from the village towards the Royal Victoria Hotel (on your left) until you reach a mini roundabout, with a finger point signpost handily sending you right, along Victoria Terrace. ❶ Follow this narrow road for 300m until it becomes an even narrower (but still tarmacked) track which quickly begins to steepen. A lot! Take your time here. This is actually one of the steepest parts of the whole walk, and you'll do yourself no favours knackering yourself out in the first half hour of the day. Bring your pace right down to that of a snail.

Keep heading uphill around the bends until you reach the Penceunant Isaf café on your left, your last sign of civilisation for a while. Carry on winding your way uphill, looking out to your left for views back down to Llanberis. You'll pass some farm buildings on your right before finally getting to a well signposted footpath on your left for 'Llanberis Path'. This is where you leave the track and start going 'off-road'.

❷ Head through the metal gate and follow the well-trodden path upwards, towards a wooden gate. And relax! That's a big chunk of your climbing out the way for a while and what's ahead of you should look welcomingly flat.

The path continues parallel to the Snowdon Mountain Railway which

Prepare yourself for the (short!) slog up to Clogwyn Station along Allt Moses.

you'll cross under for the first time and, before you know it, you'll reach the Halfway House ❸, a small pit-stop selling drinks, snacks and souvenirs. It's usually only open on summer weekends and midweek in the holidays, and is so named as it's sort of the halfway marker. (It's actually a little more than halfway in distance, but in fact takes its name from being halfway in height between sea level and the summit.)

Take a break here before continuing on, along the same path. You'll soon reach Allt Moses ❹, the next steep section up to Clogwyn Station. It's a tough but relatively short stretch along a nicely stoned path so, just like at the start of the day, take your time and know that at the top of this section is the three-quarter way-mark. When the path flattens out, you'll pass beneath the railway line again and have some amazing (/scary) views down to the Llanberis Pass.

There's now less than a mile to go! ❺ You're straight into another steep (but again, relatively short) section. Keep plodding on, uphill and over the brow. When the gradient relaxes, you reach a point where three paths converge, the Snowdon Ranger path from the right and the Pyg Track from the left. This is Bwlch Glas ❻. It's worth pausing here, looking back and making a mental note of the scene, as there is often confusion on the return with walkers taking the wrong path down.

You should (hopefully) have a good view of the summit, just 500m and less than 15 minutes ahead. Continue along the obvious path to make your way to the summit area. The path becomes a staircase as you bear left to reach the summit stone. Congratulations! You're now the highest person in Wales … for a few minutes. Grab your selfie and take the time to look around.

At this point you may have noticed the large, spaceship-type building. This is Hafod Eryri, the Snowdon Summit Visitor Centre, and unsurprisingly the highest visitor centre in the UK. Here you'll find toilets, an OK café, lots of useful information boards and a chance to buy some Snowdon souvenirs but be aware that the visitor centre is only open when the Snowdon Mountain Railway operates – typically from around late Spring until the last weekend in October, and even then, only on good weather days.

When you've had your lunch and seen enough of the views, retrace your steps back along the path you came up. Keep the railway track down to your left until you reach the point I mentioned earlier, where three paths now diverge. ❻ Ignore the paths going steeply downhill to your left and right, and instead continue straight ahead, still keeping the railway track below you and to your left. The Snowdon Ranger path bears left here and crosses the railway, so if you find yourself doing that, turn around and try again. The route back is fairly straightforward and should now be familiar. You'll reach the short tunnel for Clogwyn Station followed by the steep descent of Allt Moses. Take care on the steep downhill stretches as there are plenty of trip hazards for those not paying attention. Soon you'll be back at the Halfway House, then the railway will be passing overhead and eventually you'll get to the tarmac. Turn right here and continue downhill. If you're at death's door, you can call a taxi from the café on the corner who will come and take you back to your car or you could just battle on for the final stretch down into the village. Now's your chance to pick up some souvenirs, have a pint and relax. Congratulations! You've just climbed the highest mountain in Wales.

The Pyg Track, with Yr Wyddfa's summit showing top right.

Yr Wyddfa (Snowdon) via the Pyg / Miners' Tracks

Height	1085m (3,560ft)
Total height gain	822m (2,697ft)
Distance	11.9km (7.4 miles)
Total Time	6-7 hours
Grade	MODERATE
Start / Finish	LL55 4NU or SH 647 556 or ///fast.jeeps.splashes

This route is a very different option to the Llanberis Path. While it's shorter and there's less height to climb (as you start much higher), there is considerable rocky ground to contend with (which may involve using your hands), as well as numerous steep sections and exposed drops. That aside, it's a hugely popular route and on a summer weekend you're unlikely to be on your own.

The Pyg and Miners' Tracks both begin and end at the Pen y Pass car park, at the top of the Llanberis Pass. Beware; this is not a big car park (around 70 spaces) and it's very popular (and expensive!), and for much of the main season requires pre-booking, so don't assume you can just turn up and pay.

Parking on the roads around Pen y Pass is strictly controlled for everyone's safety, so if the car park is full don't even think about trying to park on the roadside as police regularly patrol the area and tow away what they consider 'dangerously' parked vehicles. There's a large lay-by on the A498 Beddgelert road just up from the Pen y Gwryd hotel, and from here there's a permissive footpath up to Pen y Pass which will only add an hour or so onto your day.

The best option is the Park & Ride service operating from nearby Nant Peris, where there's a much larger car park and regular buses up to Pen y Pass, or even consider parking in Llanberis or Betws-y-Coed and using the same bus service. Search online for 'Snowdon Sherpa / Sherpa'r Wyddfa' for the most up to date service information.

At the entrance to the Pen y Pass car park, you'll find toilets and a small café which, if open, is worth a visit.

This walk involves going up the Pyg Track and returning along the Miners' Track. This is the most popular way, although there's really no reason why you couldn't do it in reverse. There is, however, quite a steep descent at the top end of the Miners' Track which would be an ascent if going the other way.

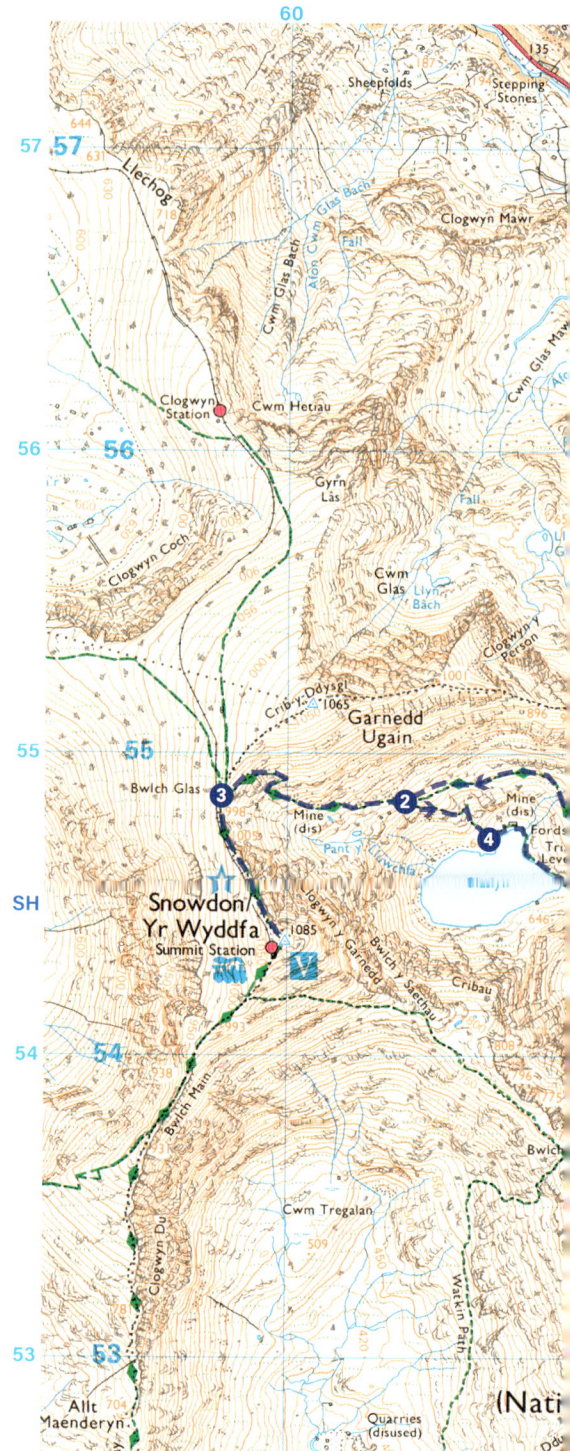

Map labels

Nant Peris

Clogwyn y Grochan

Garreg Wastad

MS 166

Bryn Du

Dinas y Gromlech

en-y-nant

Ynys Ettws

Pass of Llanberis

208

Pont y Gromlech

House Platform

Dinas Mot

Fall

Dinas Bach

MS 264

Afon Nant Peris

Cwm Beudy Mawr

Waterfall

Cwmffynnon

Llyn Cwmffynnon

387

379

Moel Berfedd

Pen-y-Gwryd Hotel

448

Start / Finish

orphwysfa

359

Pen-y-pass

344

MS

481

Tip (dis)

Craig Fach

Ysgar

Ford

A 4086

A 498

1

Bwlch y Moch

578

FBs Carreg Gwalch

Bwlch y Gwyddel

Cambrian Way

The Horns

Crib Goch

858

FB

Fall

Causeway

Afon Trawsnant

Craig Llyn Teyrn

Craig Penlan

Miners Track

Pyg Track

ord ne

FB

446

Sheepfold (dis)

Llyn Teyrn

389

Craig Penlan

Settlement

Miners Track

Level (disused)

Llyn Llydaw (Reservoir)

446

Clogwyn Pen Llechen

Afon Glaslyn

Glaslyn

FB

Cwm Dyli

Pipe Line

Sheepfolds (disused)

Falls

Works

heepfold (dis)

Craig Aderyn

314

Miners Track

Sheepfold (disused)

Sheepfold

Cattle Grid

Gwastadannas

Clogwyn Bustach

t Peak

East Peak

Y Lliwedd

Trial Level

Lliwedd Bach

Levels (disused)

Galt y Wenallt

Sheepfold (disused)

Hafod Rhisgl

Ford

FB

Tips (dis)

Mine (dis)

Falls

Afon

142

r Wyddfa (Nature Reserve)

Trial Level

FB

Falls

Level (disused)

Level (dis)

Fall

Sheepfolds

The start of the Pyg Track at Pen y Pass. Don't worry, the pointy summit (Crib Goch) is not where you're heading!

START From the Pen y Pass upper car park look for an obvious tarmac footpath leading away from the far corner. This is the start of the Pyg Track. Very quickly, the tarmac stops and the path turns into a more traditional mountain path and then into stone steps. Take your time heading up these as you don't want to wear yourself out in the first half hour. It's an obvious path, but there are a few points where you'll need to clamber over some bigger rocks. Just keep heading in the same general direction and you'll find yourself back on the path very quickly.

The mountain peak you see ahead of you is the imposing Crib Goch, but don't worry as we're going to walk around that. Stick with the path until it levels out by a stone wall at Bwlch y Moch. ❶ Here, if the weather is on your side, you'll get your first view of Llyn Llydaw and Y Lliwedd, another spectacular mountain behind it. This is a good chance to pause, have a drink and a snack. When you're ready, turn right and follow the obvious path to a stile very clearly marked 'PYG'. There is another less obvious path here that bears up to the right, which leads you to the knife-edged arête of Crib Goch. This is an exposed, grade I scramble and is not a route for beginners.

The path now continues at a much more gradual incline. Look down to your left and you'll see another path around the lake going over a causeway. That's the Miners' Track you'll be coming back along a bit later. As you keep walking, look up to your right and see if you can spot the daredevils on Crib Goch. Eventually, you'll get your first glimpse of Yr Wyddfa

Looking down the Llanberis Pass from the Pyg Track.

(Snowdon) in the distance. The path does become a little less obvious in places but is still relatively easy to follow. Take care when it narrows as the drops to your left will get increasingly dangerous. The summit is now right ahead of you.

You'll soon start climbing more steeply again and reach a large stone, marking where the Miners' Track joins from the left. ❷ Make a mental note of this spot as this is where you'll head down on your return.

The path continues with the view of the summit right ahead of you, enticing you on. It will soon become quite steep again and will zigzag a little to make the climb easier. Before you know it, you'll pop out onto the top at Bwlch Glas, where several different paths converge, with

the Snowdon Mountain Railway track in front of you. ❸ Remember this spot, as you'll need to turn here when you head back down.

It is likely to get busy now as the popular Llanberis and Snowdon Ranger paths join from the right. Turn left and you should (hopefully) have a good view of the summit just 500m and 15 minutes ahead. Continue along the obvious path adjacent to the railway track as you make your way to the summit area. Finally, the path becomes a staircase as you bear left to reach the summit stone. Congratulations!

When you've seen enough of the views, retrace your steps back along the path you came up on, keeping the railway track on your left, until you reach the point mentioned earlier, where the three paths

The Pyg Track continues ahead while the Miners' Track descends steeply to the right.

now diverge. ❸ If you parked in Llanberis and took the Park & Ride to Pen y Pass, you can continue straight ahead here and return via the Llanberis Path (Route 8).

To stay on Route 9, follow the steps down steeply to your right to re-join the Pyg Track. Take your time heading down and smile at all the people still climbing and asking, "Are we nearly there yet?" Keep going around the zigzag until you reach the split in the path where you're going to take the steep path down to the right ❷.

You're now on the Miners' Track, which descends steeply down to and around Glaslyn (blue lake). The path here isn't quite as good as the Pyg Track you came up along, but it's still pretty obvious where to go. You should be able to see the path you're aiming for ahead of you so have a bit of fun with your route choice.

❹ Once you reach the lakeside, follow the path around to the left as it continues downhill to Llyn Llydaw, the lake that you saw earlier from above. You'll pass some old mining ruins on your left as you walk around the lake, eventually crossing a causeway. It's a nice (long) easy walk back to the car park now, and before you know it, you'll see the Pen y Pass youth hostel ahead, and you're back at the start point.

Ben Nevis, seen from Càrn Mòr Dearg.

Ben Nevis, Scottish Highlands

Height	1,345m (4,413ft)
Total height gain	1,336m (4,383ft)
Distance	15.5km (9.6 miles)
Total time	8 hours
Grade	HARD
Start / Finish	PH33 6SX or NN 123 730 or ///reduce.incurring.verges

Ben Nevis is the highest mountain in the British Isles and attracts over 125,000 walkers a year. In good weather, in the height of summer, with no snow on the summit plateau, and with plenty of other walkers around, Ben Nevis isn't an especially difficult mountain to reach the top of. There's a well-trodden, easy to navigate path all the way up. However, the summit can often be under snow and access to it brings you very close to some dangerous terrain. This is definitely a mountain walk that you need to undertake with care. Our route takes you up the Mountain Path (This is sometimes called the Pony Track and historically the Tourist Path, but locals are keen to move away from that name as it wrongly gives the impression that it's suitable for anyone).

The nearest town is Fort William which is surprisingly well connected to the south. It's about a two-and-a-half-hour drive north of Glasgow, along some of the most amazing roads and through some of the most beautiful scenery. If you've seen the Bond movie, Skyfall, you'll have an idea what to expect. This is not a journey to be rushed, but rather one to be enjoyed.

An even more special journey can be had on the Caledonian Sleeper, the overnight rail service from London and the North West of England to Fort William. I've taken this train a number of times and it really is an experience. Boarding the train at a deserted London Euston in the early evening, and then waking up the next morning as the train makes its way through the most stunning Scottish scenery before arriving at Fort William for breakfast. It's not a particularly cheap way to travel, and you can struggle to get seats / berths around summer weekends, but definitely a journey I'd recommend everyone takes at least once.

The town of Fort William isn't perhaps as nice as it once was, with the town centre looking more run down with every visit (not unlike many town centres around the UK, I suppose). Nonetheless, there are plenty of accommodation options in and around the town, as well as supermarkets and various food outlets. They even have a McDonalds!

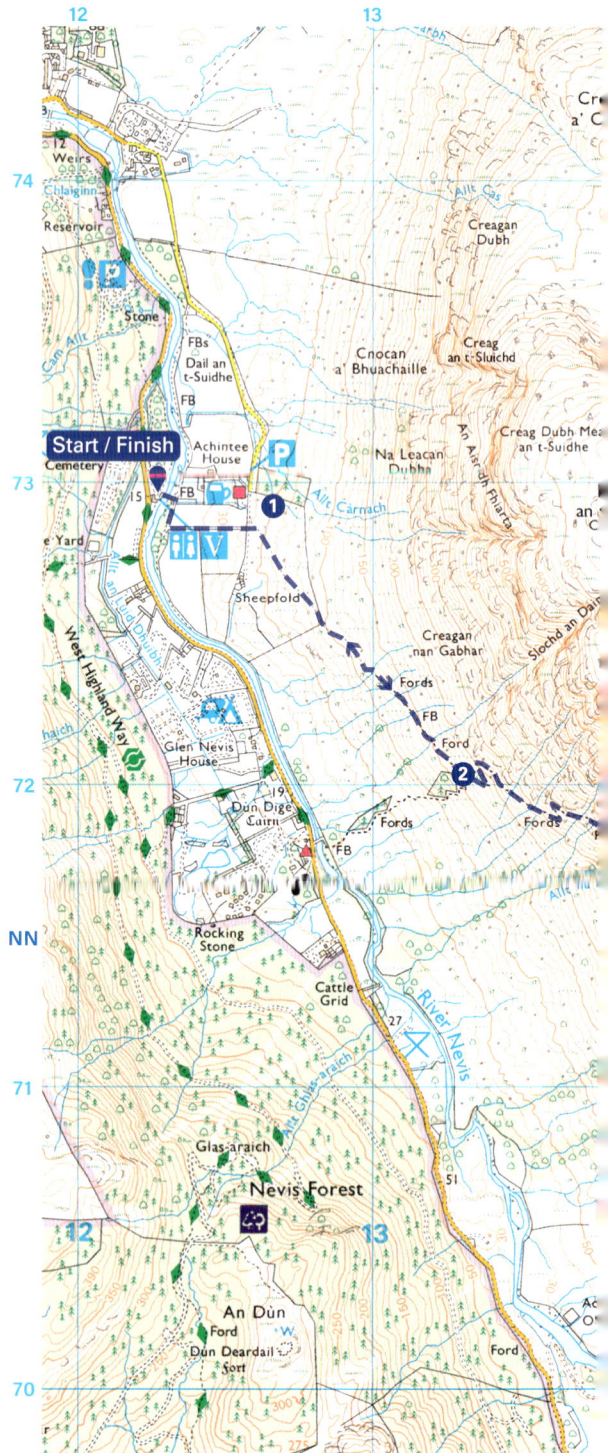

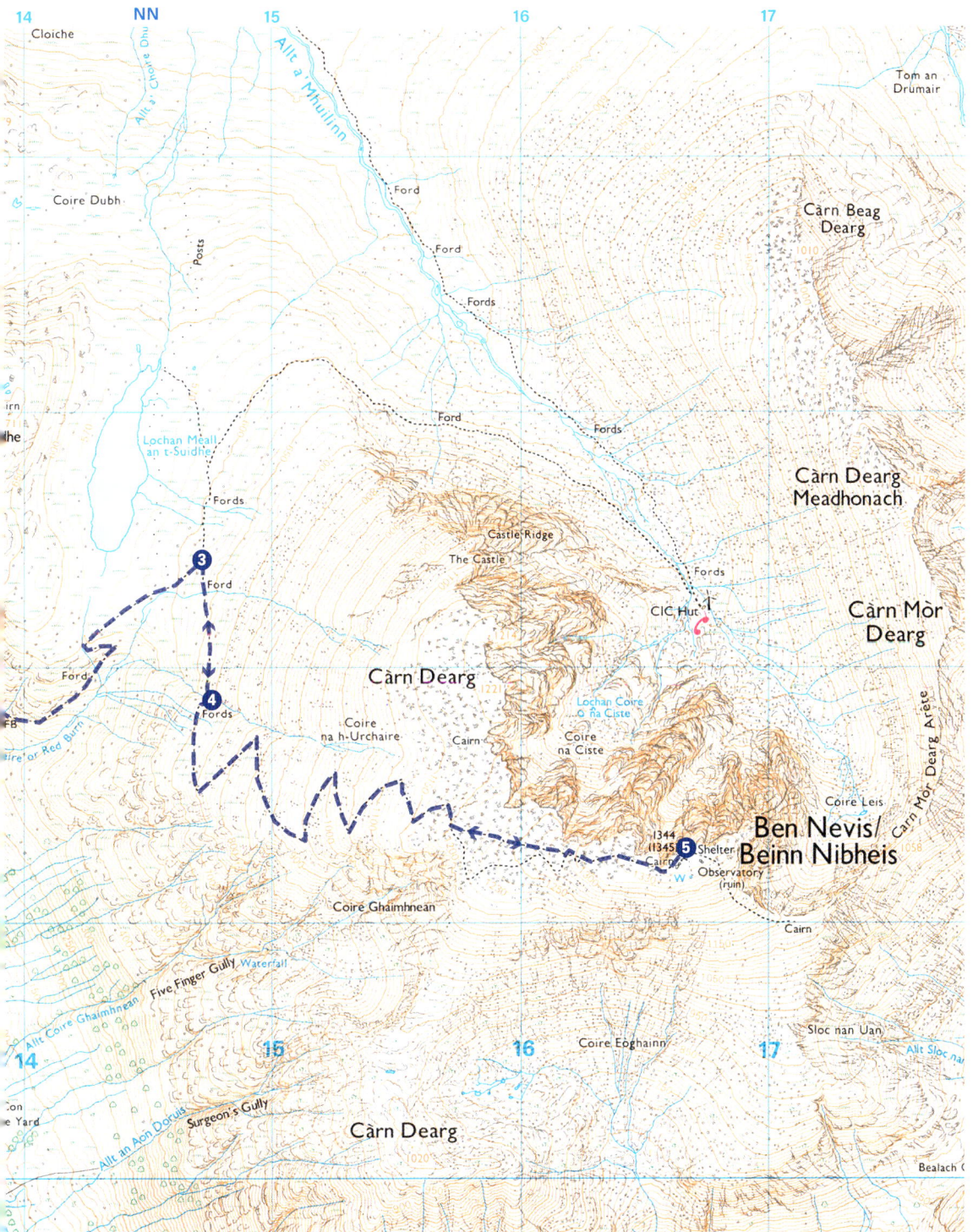

Our start point for the walk is a couple of miles outside the town, at the Ben Nevis Visitor Centre where there is parking available, providing you arrive early. A local bus runs in the summer months from the bus station in Fort William to Glen Nevis for the visitor centre. There are toilet facilities here (the last you'll see all day).

🏃 **START** Head to the back of the car park towards the visitor centre and skirt around its left-hand-side, until you come to a footpath which leads you over the River Nevis. After crossing the bridge turn right, and after around 100m turn left to cut across some fields and to join the main path up Ben Nevis. ❶ Turn right here and start your trek, gradually uphill.

Starting up the Mountain Path.
Photo: Apostolos Giontzis, Dreamstime.com

❷ After just over 1km, another path will join you from the right. This is the hostel path and if you happen to be staying at one of the nearby campsites or at the Glen Nevis Youth Hostel, this is a shortcut just for you.

The Mountain Path now doubles back on itself as you start to gain some real height. You'll cross a couple of footbridges before the path doubles back again and then starts to level out to give your legs a bit of rest. ❸ At a junction in the footpath – take the option to the right that carries on uphill. After around 500m you'll reach the cascading Red Burn ❹ – a good chance to stop and top up your water bottle.

The path now begins to zigzag, to make the climb a bit less strenuous, so take your time here. This is the toughest part of the climb, so be sure to have regular breaks, stay hydrated and eat plenty of snacks. The path will soon start to level out as you approach the summit plateau.

Assuming there's no snow around, it's a fairly simple, straight-line walk to the summit area, however, be very aware of the big drops to your left. You may be lucky enough to see rock climbers coming over the top, but give this whole area a wide berth, particularly if there is snow on the ground as cornices (overhanging edges of snow caused by the wind) are extremely dangerous. The ground near the cliff edges might look solid but it could just be a build-up of snow, so stay well back.

Beware, the summit of Ben Nevis can be snow-covered for much of the year.   *Photo: Tom Swinhoe*

It should also be said that if, as you get closer to the summit area, visibility is poor due to fog or snow then you should turn back at this point as the risks to novice mountain climbers are simply too high.

5 The summit area is a large, stony, flat plateau but avoid detouring too far from the 'middle' as the drops around you are big, and this is especially the case if there is snow on the ground. The highest point is marked by a white trig point atop a stony cairn. Once you reach this, you'll be the highest person in the United Kingdom!

Take your time to appreciate the views, take some photos and look for the ruined walls of the 19th century observatory and nearby storm shelter. It's unlikely you'll be on your own up there, so finding somewhere quiet for lunch might not be easy. Remember to stay well clear of the cliffs on three sides.

When you're refuelled and ready to head down, you'll need to retrace your steps carefully in a south-westerly direction. It should be simple enough if there is a line of people coming up, and tracks in the snow should also assist, but remember to stay well away from the steep drops and possible snow cornices now to your right. There are several large cairns that can also help guide you off the summit.

Experienced mountain walkers will use compass bearings to find their way back to the Mountain Path in poor visibility, but as novice walkers you should not allow yourself to get into this situation. I cannot stress enough that approaching

Looking down on Lochan Meall an t-Suidhe from the Mountain Path.   *Photo: Josefkubes, Dreamstime.com*

the summit plateau in bad weather or anything that restricts your visibility is extremely dangerous and you should have turned back. It's very easy for things to go very wrong. If you're at all unsure of your abilities or of the weather conditions, consider hiring a local guide.

Once you've reached the Mountain Path, the journey down is the same route you took up, just with different views. The zigzags will take away a good amount of height and you'll soon reach the Red Burn again. ❹ After crossing the burn, you'll walk over a fairly flat area for just over 500m before you need to take the path to your left to continue downhill. ❸ Be careful not to miss this path junction as carrying straight on will lead you into some difficult terrain. The path descends gradually and then more steeply as you zigzag around the steepest parts, and soon you'll be back at the junction with the hostel path. If you're camping locally or staying at the Ben Nevis Youth Hostel you can turn left here, down the hostel path, otherwise continue onwards.

The descent becomes much more gradual, and you'll soon reach the path across the field marked by a stone cairn. Cross the field, turn right at the treeline, then left over the river and back to the car park.

Cadair Ìdris with Llyn Cau in the foreground

Route 10

Cadair Idris, Eryri (Snowdonia)

Height	893m (2,930ft)
Total height gain	950m (3,117ft)
Distance	9km (5.6 miles)
Total time	4.5-5 hours
Grade	HARD
Start / Finish	LL36 9AJ or SH 732 115 or ///warmers.lighters.reports

Cadair Idris is a spectacular peak at the southern end of the Snowdonia National Park, and the highest point in mid-Wales. It might not be as popular as Snowdon but it's still a busy mountain, particularly with school groups and charity challenges (and it makes up one of the Welsh Three Peaks).

The valleys around Cadair Idris are part of the Mach Loop where fast jets from the RAF and US Air Force routinely practise low-level flying, so don't be shocked when you hear / see planes flying beneath you.

There are a few route options available. The most popular, and my favourite, is the Minffordd Path which is the shortest but

In the early stages, the route is well marked.

also the steepest. It begins in beautiful woodland, before transforming into a magnificent open valley with your target mountain right in front of you. Whichever way you decide to come down is tough going, so take your time.

The walk starts from the Dol Idris car park just off the A487. It's a good-sized car park but, as with all parking in popular walking spots, it will fill up quickly on busy days. TrawsCymru operates a regular bus from Bangor in the north to Aberystwyth in mid-Wales that stops at Minffordd. With some careful planning this can make climbing Cadair Idris by public transport very doable.

START Exit the car park from the far end, just past the toilets, and head through the kissing gate, turning right along the wooded path. The actual Minffordd Path begins where the path bears left in front of the five-bar gate. Continue through the next kissing gate and past the Tŷ Te Cadair Tea Room, which is well worth a drop in on your way back. ❶ Shortly after the tea room you'll cross over a stream, then look out for a gate on your right signposted 'Cader Idris' (Cader is how you'll sometimes see Cadair written). Pass through the gate and start climbing.

The path gets steeper as you continue through the trees, and you begin to get a real taste of what's to come. Follow the steps as they wind through the forest with the stream on your right, until you eventually emerge into open terrain with a magnificent view of Cadair Idris ahead of you.

❷ Stay left at an intersection in the path signed Cwm Cau (the right-hand option is your return route) and keep heading uphill. You'll bear round to your left gradually and the inclines will soon level out for some respite as you approach Llyn Cau (a great wild swimming spot). Here you are rewarded with a full view of the mountain you're going to climb.

❸ As you approach the lake there's a short path to the right that leads to the waterfront – this is a lovely spot to have a snack but if you want to keep going then ignore this, keep left and continue steeply uphill. As you approach the top of this section there are fabulous views down into the valley to your left, where you'll frequently see fighter jets training below you. ❹ The path is still pretty good up here, but it essentially just keeps going around to your right with the steep drops down to Llyn Cau also on your right.

You should soon be able to see Penygadair which marks the summit of Cadair Idris over to the right, but you'll also note there's quite a large 'dip' in between. Unfortunately, you need to descend around 100m into Craig Cau (take care here as it's quite rocky) before you start your final ascent to the summit.

The summit is a very obvious high point, with a familiar trig point atop a pile of stones but if you lose sight of it at all keep following the cairns. It's a bit of a rocky climb towards the end but just keep heading uphill.

❺ The Pony Path (another popular ascent route) joins from the left just before the summit, so expect to see another line of walkers arriving from that direction.

Take some time to admire the views here. You're at the highest point in mid-Wales with mountains all around you.

You now have a choice to make. To enjoy a circular walk we're going to carry on along the ridge ahead of you to Mynydd Moel, and then descend on the other side to re-join the path we came up. However, this section of the route is less obvious, and you'll be walking away from footpaths in places so it should only be attempted in good visibility and if you're confident of your abilities. If you're at all unsure, then an equally common way back is to simply retrace the path you took up.

If you're up for the challenge, head off along the ridge following a faint foot-path of sorts. It's a relatively flat, but sometimes boggy, section all the way to Mynydd Moel and easy to follow as you're on top of a ridge. Use the stile to cross over the fence just before the sum-mit, which is marked by a small stone shelter and offers amazing views in all directions. Be aware that there are some steep drops here.

❻ The route down is much less obvi-ous and you can do one of two things. If you're at all unsure or the visibility isn't great, then retrace your steps back to the fence you crossed 100m back along the ridge and turn left, downhill, keeping the fence on your right. Alternatively, keeping those very steep drops behind you and the ridge you've just been walking along to your right, start walking downhill to-wards the fence line further down. This fence is your guide home so, whichever way you choose, once you reach it follow it downhill.

The steps up through the forest are a real sign of what's to come, with plenty more climbing ahead.

The gradient varies and it does get a little rough in places, but as long as you're with the fence you're safe. While there's no official path here it's obvious there have been attempts at path-building in the past and it's easy enough to follow. Ignore the first stile you come across. Carry on along the fence until you reach another ❼, which will lead you to a path that descends back into the valley. Cross the stream over a makeshift slate bridge and re-join the path we started on at the intersection. Turn left here and retrace your steps back down into the woodland and to the car park.

A mother and son descending to Wasdale on a hot summer day.

Scafell Pike looming in the distance.

Route 11

Scafell Pike, Lake District

Height	978m (3,209ft)
Total height gain	908m (2,979ft)
Distance	9km (5.6 miles)
Total time	5-6 hours
Grade	HARD
Start / Finish	CA20 1EX or NY 187 085 or ///currently.switched.tile

Scafell Pike in the Lake District is the highest mountain in England. It is perhaps the lesser known of the 'Three Peaks' and should never be shortened to 'Scafell', as that's a different peak nearby. It's also more difficult to reach than Snowdon or Ben Nevis. Not because of its height (it's around 100m lower than Snowdon and 350m lower than Ben Nevis) but because of its lesser-trodden, numerous routes which can make navigation more difficult. However, like all the routes in this book, with the right conditions, the right equipment and the right team it's perfectly doable.

Getting to the start point in the tiny Lake District hamlet of Wasdale Head is the first challenge. It's around a 90-minute drive off the M6, through some beautiful

The summit of Scafell Pike is an ankle-breaking pile of rocks. Take care!

but winding mountain roads that will challenge even the most experienced country driver. There's a small parking area on the village green for around 50 cars, and on busy summer weekends a local farmer opens a field for extra capacity. Please park responsibly, showing consideration for the locals. Further into the hamlet is the famous Wasdale Head Inn which claims to be the birthplace of British climbing. It offers hotel and self-catering accommodation as well as a campsite, and the bar and restaurant are definitely worth a visit. There's also a small outdoor shop in case you've left something at home.

There have been various public transport options in the past that come and go with demand, but in reality coming by car is your only choice here.

START From the 'car park' turn left and walk a short distance along the road until it bears right. At this point you'll see two gates to your left. Cross over the left-hand stile and follow the faint path, moving away from the fence line into the trees ahead. The path becomes more obvious through the trees and eventually comes to a footbridge over Lingmell Beck. ❶ Immediately after the footbridge, turn right and pass through the kissing gate. The path starts climbing gradually now as we skirt around the hillside. Take your time here as it's going to get tougher ahead.

Pass through another kissing gate and bear left. The views to your right down to Wast Water are spectacular on a good day. You'll soon reach Lingmell Gill ❷, and the path bears left here taking you into

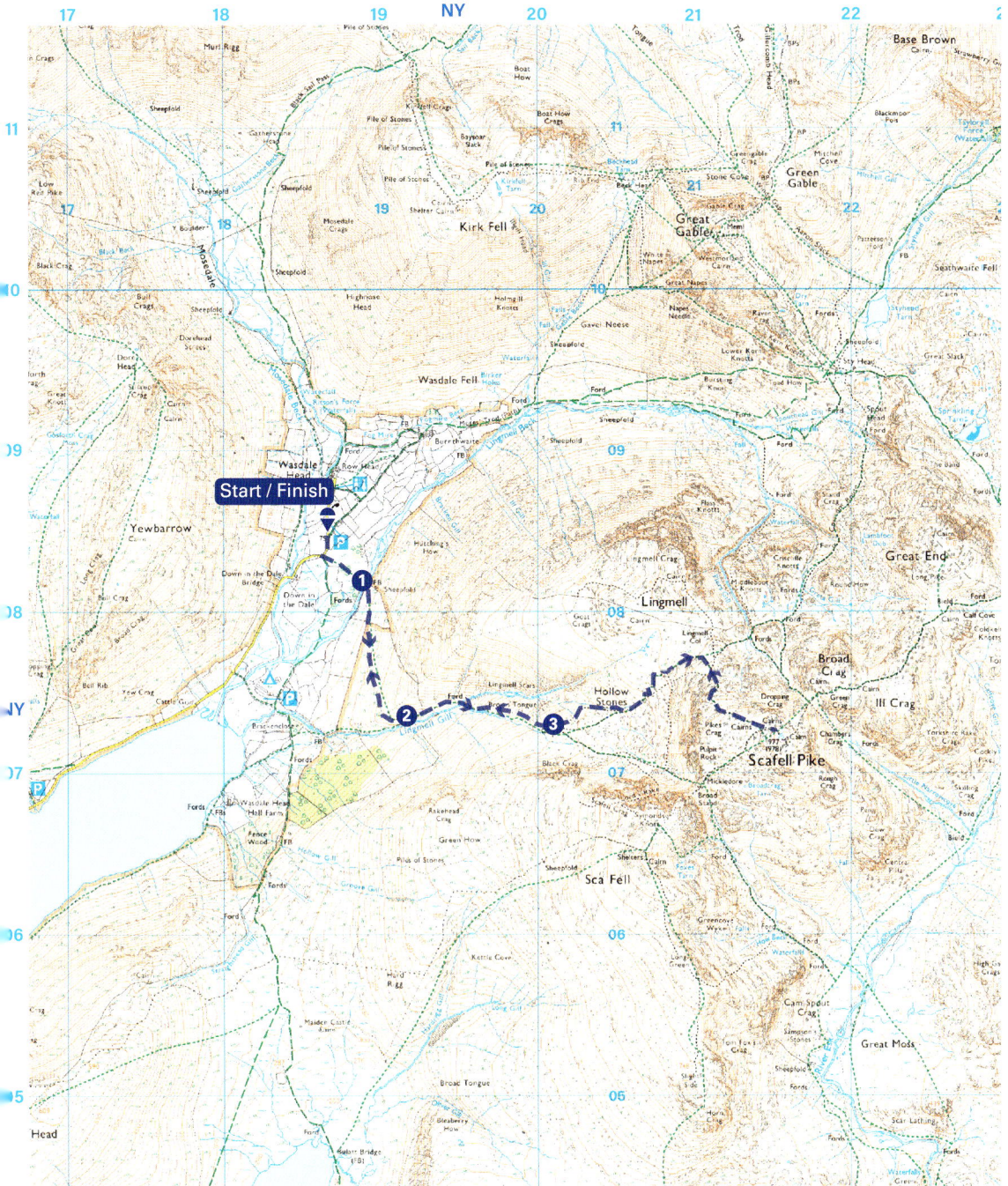

Map created by Lovell Johns Limited. Based upon Ordnance Survey digital map data

© Crown Copyright 2023 Licence Number 43368U. All rights reserved.

Take care starting your descent from the summit, be sure you're heading in the right direction.

the valley, where eventually you'll cross the stream. Take care here as, even after the smallest amount of rainfall, the water will have some power. Pick your route across, then join the stone path as the incline starts to steepen. The path is now much more obvious, so just keep going.

❸ As you're plodding up the steps, you'll reach a fork in the path where you'll need to take the left-hand option. It'll start to zigzag at the really steep bits, as it steers you round those big crags to your right. You'll soon find yourself on top of those crags as the path becomes considerably rockier. Take extra care when walking over these rocks as foot and ankle injuries are easy to come by. The slog continues but now you can see your destination ahead in the distance. At this point, just keep following the path 'upwards' to the highest point. The summit plateau is a huge mass of rocks. Look out for the trig point and shelter directly ahead and then take your time to admire the views. Take care here to note the direction you're approaching from, as you'll need to find this path down again, and the rocky plateau can make this tricky.

Just like the other two of our 'National Three Peaks', it's unlikely you'll be at the summit on your own. It can feel a bit crowded as you congregate with walkers who have come up other paths from all around you. However, it's quite a large summit area so you don't have to go far to find a quieter spot to rest for a short while. Just be sure to keep your bearings about you, and an eye on the path you came up on as that's your way down as well.

When you've caught your breath, had some refreshments and taken some photos, it's time to head back. The return route is the reversal of the way you came up. The scenery will look different so you should take care to make sure you're on the right path.

There are two 'more obvious' paths down. With your back to the shelter, you want to be walking in a north-west direction. I say 'more obvious' as the paths can be difficult to see, so look out for the different colour rocks and keep an eye out for the path in the distance. If you were to draw an imaginary straight line from the shelter to the trig point and then continue it on, that would be the general direction to head in. The seaside resort of Seascale and the Irish Sea should be visible in the distance, slightly to your left. You should re-join an actual path very quickly. Here there's a series of cairns (piles of rocks used to guide people in poor visibility), so you can just keep heading to the next one.

The path is pretty straight for about 500m, then bears right and then left again as you skirt around the crags you passed on your way up. Take extra care coming down here, as the scree can be loose in places and legs might be getting tired. Keep going through the short zigzag area, past the path junction and eventually you'll end up back at the water crossing. You're more than halfway back now.

After you've carefully crossed Lingmell Gill, carry on parallel to the stream before bearing right after the kissing gate. This path will take you back to the footbridge over Lingmell Beck. Cross here and walk in a straight line across the fields until you get back to the road, where you turn right for the short stretch back to the start point.

Anyone can climb a mountain! A charity walker at the summit of Yr Wyddfa (Snowdon).

Useful Resources

Websites

AdventureSmart – www.adventuresmart.uk

Darebee – www.darebee.com

Database of British and Irish Hills – www.hill-bagging.co.uk

Met Office Mountain Weather Forecasts
– www.metoffice.gov.uk/weather/specialist-forecasts/mountain

Mountain Weather Information Service (MWIS) – www.mwis.org.uk

National Parks UK – www.nationalparks.uk

The Countryside Code – www.gov.uk/government/publications/the-countryside-code

Trail 100 – www.livefortheoutdoors.com/trail-100

Traveline – www.traveline.info

Traveline Cymru – www.traveline.cymru

Books

Adventure Revolution, Belinda Kirk, Piatkus, 2021, ISBN 9780349428239

Britain's Highest Mountain Walks, Jeremy Ashcroft, Collins, 2013,
ISBN 9780007488216

Heights of Madness, Jonny Muir, John Blake, 2009, ISBN 9781844546640

Hillwalking, Steve Long, Mountain Training UK, 2014, ISBN 9780954151195

Mountain and Moorland Navigation, Kevin Walker, Pesda Press, 2016,
ISBN 9781906095567

Navigation Skills for Walkers, Terry Marsh, Ordnance Survey, 2019,
ISBN 9780319091753

Outdoor First Aid, Katherine Wills, Pesda Press, 2013, ISBN 9781906095352

The Ultimate Navigation Manual, Lyle Brotherton, Collins, 2011, ISBN 9780007424603

The UK's County Tops, Jonny Muir, Cicerone Press, 2011, ISBN 9781852846299

Publications

Country Walking – www.countrywalking.co.uk

Countryfile Magazine – www.countryfile.com/magazine

The Great Outdoors – www.thegreatoutdoorsmag.com

Grough – www.grough.co.uk/magazine

Trail Magazine – www.trailmagazine.com

UKClimbing – www.ukclimbing.com

UKHillwalking – www.ukhillwalking.com

Organisations

British Orienteering – www.britishorienteering.org.uk

The British Mountaineering Council – www.thebmc.co.uk

British Mountain Guides (IFMGA) – www.bmg.org.uk

British Walking Federation – www.bwf-ivv.org.uk

Hostelling International NI – www.hini.org.uk

Hostelling Scotland – www.hostellingscotland.org.uk

Meetup – www.meetup.com

Mountain Bothies Association – www.mountainbothies.org.uk

Mountain Rescue England and Wales – www.mountain.rescue.org.uk

Mountain Training – www.mountain-training.org

Mountaineering Scotland – www.mountaineering.scot

National Navigation Award Scheme – www.nnas.org.uk

Ordnance Survey – www.ordnancesurvey.co.uk

OutdoorLads – www.outdoorlads.com

The Ramblers – www.ramblers.org.uk

Scottish Mountain Rescue – www.scottishmountainrescue.org

YHA England & Wales – www.yha.org.uk

Glossary

AdventureSmart – An outdoor safety campaign (see Chapter 6, The Countryside Code).

bagging – Reaching a peak or summit. A term typically used by those climbing a collection of hills or mountains.

blister – A bubble on the skin usually caused by friction or heat.

bog – An area of wet or muddy ground.

bothy – A small shelter usually found in remote Scottish mountains.

bridleway – A route that can be used by cyclists and horse riders as well as pedestrians.

Buff – A brand of face covering used to keep the wind and cold off your face.

burn – A Scottish term for a large stream or river.

byway – A route open to vehicles (but not a public road).

cairn – A man-made pile of rocks or stones, often used to help navigate off a mountain in poor visibility.

col (or saddle) – The low point between two hills.

compass – A device with a magnetised pointer showing the direction of magnetic north.

contour – A line on a map indicating height.

Corbett – A mountain in Scotland with a height between 2,500 and 3,000ft.

crag – A rocky formation, often home to rock climbers.

crampons – Spikes attached to your walking boots to help you move on snow and ice without slipping.

CRoW Act – Colloquially known as the 'Right to Roam', it is an Act of Parliament affecting England and Wales giving walkers permission to use open access land without the need to stick rigidly to public footpaths.

Countryside Code, The – Guidance issued on behalf of the UK Government on how visitors to the countryside should behave.

fell – A Lake District term for a hill or mountain.

fingerpost – A type of sign often found in the countryside to indicate directions of different paths.

footpath – A route usually intended for pedestrians only (i.e., not for cyclists).

ford – A shallow spot in a river or stream enabling walkers to cross.

gaiters – Covers for the top of your boots to help keep your feet dry.

Glossary

Goretex – A trade name for a waterproof, breathable membrane used in a good deal of outdoor gear to help the wearer stay dry.

grid reference – A set of letters and numbers used to pinpoint an exact location on a map.

ice axe – A metal tool used to help winter mountaineers ascend and descend on snow and ice.

kissing gate – A means for people (but not animals) to cross a boundary such as a fence or wall. The hinged gate swings back and forth.

livestock – Animals raised in an agricultural environment such as sheep or cows.

llyn – A Welsh word for lake.

moor – An area of open land.

Munro – A mountain in Scotland above 3,000ft.

National Trail – A route specifically created for walking, horse riding and cycling.

open access – Allows you to explore away from paths (see CRoW Act).

permissive footpath – Sometimes called a concessionary path, a route that the landowner permits use of by the public, although not a public right of way.

personal locator beacon (PLB) – A device designed to emit a distress signal to summon help at sea or in the mountains.

purification tablets – Used for turning naturally found water into drinking water.

scrambling – The 'grey area' between hill walking and rock climbing. Expect to use your hands even on easy scrambles.

stile – A (usually wooden) feature for crossing a boundary such as a fence or wall. Used instead of gates to ensure animals can't escape.

summit – The top of the mountain you're climbing.

tor – Old English name for a hill or peak.

tarn – A small mountain lake.

trig point – A concrete pillar (usually painted white) found at high points such as on top of hills. Originally used by Ordnance Survey to help map the country.

Wainwrights – A collection of Lake District peaks made famous by guidebook author Alfred Wainwright. A popular activity amongst some is to walk all 214 Wainwrights.

wild camping – Setting up camp anywhere other than an official campsite.

TRAIL 100 PEAK BAGGER'S CHART

Here's your downloadable planner for the *Trail 100*. Hand-picked by the experts at *Trail* magazine, it's a bucket list collection of the 100 UK peaks all hillwalkers must climb at least once in their life. Tick and date the ones you've climbed, then start planning the ones you haven't!

SCOTLAND

THE HIGHLANDS

Peak	Height	Grid Ref	Description	
▲ Ben Nevis	1345m	NN166712	Britain's highest peak; a stunning, complex labyrinth of routes for all.	
▲ Ben Lawers NEW 2020	1214m	NN635414	Bag a Munro from the 500m car park or as part of a glorious multi-peak traverse.	
▲ Ben More NEW 2020	1174m	NN433244	Sadistically steep, perfectly triangular; it dominates the skyline.	
▲ Bidean nam Bian	1150m	NN143542	A fortress of a mountain, closeted and grand – the highest in Glen Coe.	
▲ Ben Alder	1148m	NN496717	Fiercely remote and hard-won, but impressive and satisfying with it.	
▲ Ben Lui	1130m	NN265263	Tall, elegant gatekeeper to the Highlands, defined by amazing north-east corrie.	
▲ Ben Cruachan	1126m	NN069303	A massive presence, once thought to be Scotland's highest peak.	
▲ Sgurr a' Mhaim	1099m	NN164667	Quartzite-topped spur on the Mamores' thrilling Ring of Steall horseshoe.	
▲ Schiehallion	1083m	NN714547	Scientifically important for its symmetry; a wonderful mountain besides.	
▲ Sgurr Fhuaran	1067m	NG978166	Central of Kintail's Five Sisters. West ridge a stunningly sustained ascent.	
▲ An Teallach	1060m	NH063837	Brutally built and terrifyingly sheer; probably our scariest walker's peak.	
▲ Liathach	1055m	NG929579	Dominates Torridon like an open bear trap. An awesome expedition.	
▲ Sgurr na Ciche	1040m	NM902966	Fantastically remote, rough, tough cone on the edge of Knoydart.	
▲ Buachaille Etive Mor	1022m	NN222542	Sentinel of Glen Coe; star of a million postcards. Demanding as a climb.	
▲ Ladhar Bheinn	1020m	NG821041	Isolated and complex king of the Knoydart wilderness. One of the best.	
▲ Beinn Eighe	1010m	NG951611	Immense... a circle of Munro summits enclosing an ancient corrie.	
▲ The Saddle	1010m	NG934130	Mighty and sharp, climbing this Glen Shiel hulk via Forcan Ridge is a must.	
▲ Beinn Alligin	986m	NG865613	Charismatic, satisfying and home to Britain's hardest-won views.	
▲ Slioch NEW 2020	981m	NH005689	Stands like a castle keep over Loch Maree. Impressive in every way.	
▲ Ben Lomond	974m	NN367028	Most southerly Munro, many people's first. Scenically stupendous.	
▲ A' Mhaighdean	967m	NH008749	One of the UK's remotest peaks, part of a fearsome northern wilderness.	
▲ Ben Hope	927m	NC478501	Most northerly Munro, magical and isolated on the northern coast.	
▲ Foinaven	911m	NC315507	Bulky, northern ridge walk with incredible views and precipitous screes.	
▲ Beinn Dearg Mor	906m	NH032799	Remote and dramatic neighbour to An Teallach. Compact but spectacular.	
▲ Garbh Bheinn	885m	NM904622	Unexploited and breathlessly rugged... a gem of a rough diamond.	
▲ The Cobbler	884m	NN259058	Collapsed, tortured jumble of a peak with a thrilling summit block.	
▲ Quinag	808m	NC209292	A flail of contours from above, underfoot a stunning set of walker's ridges.	
▲ Suilven	731m	NC153183	Fantastically weird, utterly unique and set in a special part of Scotland.	
▲ Stac Pollaidh	612m	NC107106	Ragged little peak; great scrambling and views that belie its accessibility.	

GALLOWAY

Peak	Height	Grid Ref	Description	
▲ Merrick	843m	NX427855	The highest point in a fascinating zone of incredibly rough uplands.	

CAIRNGORMS

Peak	Height	Grid Ref	Description	
▲ Ben Macdui	1309m	NN988989	Brooding and sprawling, Britain's deputy is a wilderness of a mountain.	
▲ Braeriach NEW 2020	1296m	NN953999	A remote Cairngorm colossus; a wild, vast and dramatic plateau.	
▲ Lochnagar	1155m	NO243861	Scotland's eastern giant; half sub-Arctic plateau, half vertical cliff.	
▲ The Devil's Point NEW 2020	1004m	NN976951	At the junction of two epic glens; the most striking viewpoint in the Cairngorms.	

SCOTTISH ISLANDS

Peak	Height	Grid Ref	Description	
▲ Sgurr Alasdair	992m	NG450207	Highest on Skye; a scrambly ridge takes you into the heart of the Cuillin.	
▲ Sgurr Dearg	986m	NG444215	The 'Inaccessible Pinnacle'. A V Diff climb, but a hell of an ambition.	
▲ Ben More	966m	NM525330	High point of Mull, a Munro that is often left until last due to its location.	
▲ Sgurr nan Gillean	964m	NG471252	Cuillin end-stop is horned and scary-looking; easiest way up is a scramble.	
▲ Bla Bheinn	928m	NG530218	Skye's most impressive single mountain, and a stunning objective.	
▲ Goatfell	874m	NR991415	Sharp centrepiece to Arran's underrated and dramatic highlands.	
▲ Askival	812m	NM393952	Most satisfying peak on the utterly extraordinary island of Rum.	
▲ Beinn an Oir	785m	NR498749	One of Jura's 'Paps' – three unique mountains on this sequestered isle.	

N IRELAND

Peak	Height	Grid Ref	Description	
▲ Slieve Donard	850m	J358276	Highest point in Northern Ireland, and a fine figurehead for the Mournes.	

BROUGHT TO YOU BY
komoot
SCARPA
Lowe alpine

Full peak descriptions and downloadable route guides at:
lfto.com/trail100

ENGLAND

LAKE DISTRICT

▲ Scafell Pike	978m	NY215072	England's highest point; complex, indefinable, essential and satisfying.	☐
▲ Sca Fell	964m	NY205065	Brooding and grand, sees a fraction of the traffic of its noisy neighbour.	☐
▲ Helvellyn	950m	NY341151	Striking 3000ft plateau bitten by walkable arêtes of exceptional quality.	☐
▲ Skiddaw	931m	NY260290	Massive and bare; dominates the northern Lakes. Strikingly good views.	☐
▲ Bow Fell	902m	NY244064	Muscular and feature-packed; ranks among England's very best.	☐
▲ Great Gable	899m	NY212103	A labyrinth of crags, gullies and cliffs; drips with history and atmosphere.	☐
▲ Pillar	892m	NY171121	Magnificently set, and packed with interest including historic Pillar Rock.	☐
▲ Fairfield	873m	NY358117	Grand centrepiece of its namesake horseshoe. Perfect for first-timers.	☐
▲ Blencathra	868m	NY323277	Imposing classic, home to superb spurs Sharp Edge and Hall's Fell Ridge.	☐
▲ Grasmoor	852m	NY174203	Bulky Buttermere giant; overlooked and secluded, its top is magisterial.	☐
▲ St Sunday Crag	841m	NY369134	Engaging outlier of Fairfield, home to necky (and optional) Pinnacle Ridge.	☐
▲ High Street	828m	NY440110	Plateau with a superb eastern ascent. Few Lakeland hills feel this huge.	☐
▲ High Stile	806m	NY167147	Shapely peak and a marvellous, chiselled traverse off the beaten track.	☐
▲ The Old Man of Coniston	803m	SD272978	Southern fells classic; industry-scarred, but rugged and unbowed.	☐
▲ Grisedale Pike	791m	NY198225	Sharp, far-flung and a magical viewpoint, the best summit of the Coledale Round.	☐
▲ Glaramara	783m	NY246104	Seemingly gentle hill with wonderful, scrambly ground on top.	☐
▲ Wetherlam	762m	NY288011	Charismatic hill with great views and greenery to the north and east.	☐
▲ Ill Bell NEW 2020	757m	NY436077	Craggy top on the wonderful rollercoaster that is the Kentmere Horseshoe.	☐
▲ Pike of Stickle	709m	NY274073	Ancient and distinctive highlight of the Langdale Pikes. Utterly unique.	☐
▲ Place Fell	657m	NY405169	Often overlooked; rocky and magnificent viewpoint above Ullswater.	☐
▲ Yewbarrow	628m	NY173085	Striking and challenging prow above Wast Water; distinctive and grand.	☐
▲ Black Combe	600m	SD135854	Outlier of Lakeland; the perfect bridge between land and sea.	☐
▲ Haystacks	597m	NY193131	Achingly pretty setting; Wainwright's most beloved hill.	☐
▲ Cat Bells NEW 2020	451m	NY244198	At only 451m tall, it's every bit a mountain in character, with huge views.	☐
▲ Helm Crag	405m	NY327093	Dumpling of a hill with a ratty, terrifying summit block. A test of nerves.	☐

NORTHERN PENNINES

▲ The Cheviot	815m	NT908205	Terminus of the Pennine Way is very wild; splendid for lovers of moors.	☐
▲ Cross Fell	893m	NY687343	Weather-battered Pennine giant; England's highest outside Lakes.	☐

YORKSHIRE DALES

▲ Ingleborough	724m	SD741745	Icon of Yorkshire; full of caves, limestone pavement and proud summit.	☐
▲ The Calf	676m	SD667970	Focal point of underrated Howgill Fells. Northern end wonderfully remote.	☐

PEAK DISTRICT

▲ Kinder Scout	636m	SK085875	Scene of the famous Mass Trespass; in winter a bleak, white wildland.	☐

NORTH YORK MOORS

▲ Roseberry Topping	320m	NZ579125	Tooth of a hill rising above North Yorkshire; grandest thing for miles.	☐

DARTMOOR

▲ Yes Tor	619m	SX582900	Impressively high Dartmoor summit; nearby High Willhays the true top.	☐

WALES

NORTH WALES

▲ Snowdon	1085m	SH610544	Stupendous; extreme and worthy despite compromised its summit.	☐
▲ Carnedd Llewelyn	1064m	SH683644	Bulky and knurled, a fitting contrast to Snowdon. Near-polar in winter.	☐
▲ Carnedd Dafydd	1044m	SH663630	Round and comely from the south; a massive cliff to the north.	☐
▲ Glyder Fach	994m	SH656582	Lesser in height but grander in stature than Fawr. Bristly Ridge a hoot.	☐
▲ Pen yr Ole Wen NEW 2020	978m	SH655619	The impressive western-front of the Carneddau, with an exciting east ridge.	☐
▲ Y Garn NEW 2020	947m	SH631595	Chewed and craggy down into Cwm Idwal; it's a worthy Glyderau 3000 er.	☐
▲ Elidir Fawr	924m	SH612613	A bold, defiant mountain despite industrial flanks and interior.	☐
▲ Crib Goch NEW 2020	923m	SH624552	Notorious knife-edge Grade 1 scramble to Snowdon. A rite of passage!	☐
▲ Tryfan	917m	SH664593	Striking, freestanding thorn of fun; perhaps Wales's finest single peak.	☐
▲ Aran Fawddwy	905m	SH862223	Overlooked – a secret mountain of great height and quality.	☐
▲ Y Lliwedd	898m	SH622533	Intimidating mirror to Crib Goch; most dramatic way off Snowdon.	☐
▲ Cadair Idris	893m	SH711130	Complex and striking, Snowdon's southern miniature is thick with legend.	☐
▲ Moel Siabod	872m	SH705546	Gateway to Snowdonia. Fun ridge and cracking views of Snowdon.	☐
▲ Moel Hebog	782m	SH565469	Jumbled, volcanic hill that is terrifically sheer from the east.	☐
▲ Yr Aran NEW 2020	747m	SH605515	Pointy outlier of Snowdon, with stunning 360° views.	☐
▲ Rhinog Fawr	720m	SH656289	Rugged, crumbling hill in the phenomenal Rhinogs range. Essential.	☐
▲ Mynydd Drws-y-coed	695m	SH548518	Best bit of the Nantlle Ridge; thrillingly airy, with satisfying scrambling.	☐
▲ Cnicht	689m	SH645466	Fantastically pointy objective above Croesor; hugely enjoyable.	☐
▲ Arenig Fach	689m	SH820243	Dull from afar, this hill rewards the intrepid with perfect Llyn Arenig Fach.	☐
▲ Maesglase	674m	SH822151	Green, delightfully different Middle Earth-ish peak with waterfall.	☐
▲ Yr Eifl NEW 2020	564m	SH365447	Walk from sea to rocky summit for 'wow' views of the entire Llyn Peninsula.	☐

CENTRAL WALES

▲ Pumlumon	752m	SN789869	Rugged, multi-topped and (currently) unspoiled mid-Wales oddball.	☐

SOUTH WALES

▲ Pen y Fan	886m	SO011215	Ever popular; a majestic, uniquely sculpted southern giant.	☐
▲ Fan Brycheiniog	802m	SN825218	The Black Mountain. Stunning; a cliff to east, sculpted valleys to north.	☐
▲ Sugar Loaf	596m	SO273187	Charismatic nipple with terrific views; gatekeeper to south Wales.	☐

CASUALTY REPORT **FORM**

Complete as much of this form as possible.
The form should remain with the casualty at all times.

	A. T. M. I. S. T. HANDOVER		
A	Age: Date of Birth: Name:		
T	Time of incident: Time \ arrived:		
M	Mechanism of injury/ Medical complaint:		
I	Injuries found/ Medical findings:		

Signs & Symptoms	Present?	Tourniquet used?
MASSIVE BLEED	**Y/ N**	**Y TIME / N**
RESPONSE	**A C V P U**	
AIRWAY	Open & Clear: **Y/ N**	
BREATHING	Rate:	
CIRCULATION	Pulse: % SPO2:	
TEMPERATURE	**HOT** **NORMAL** **COLD**	
Other Casualty Info:	**S. A. M. P. L. E.**	

(**S** label appears beside the Signs & Symptoms table)

T	**Treatment given:** **Medication given/taken:**

OTHER USEFUL CASUALTY INFORMATION

S Signs and Symptoms

A Allergies:

M Medications:

P Past Medical History:

L Last **IN** last **OUT**:

E Events

INFORMATION FOR MOUNTAIN RESCUE

Your mobile/telephone number: _____   Second phone number: _____

Your location: Grid Ref: _____

Description of your location: _____

How many in the group: _____   Age ranges of the group: _____   Any pre-existing medical conditions in the group: If yes detail below: _____

Clothing description of group: (i.e. colours rather than brand) _____

DIAL 999/112 request the appropriate Rescue Services

ACTIVE FIRST AID   **www.activefirstaid.co.uk**

Casualty Report Form

IMMEDIATE ACTION (PRIMARY SURVEY - ABC's)	EMERGENCY

Airway →
- **CONSCIOUS** - Clear and Open ☐
- **CONSCIOUS** - But with an Airway Problem → ☐ → **EMERGENCY: Dial 999/112**
- **UNCONSCIOUS** → Check & Open → ☐ → If they remain unconscious this is an **EMERGENCY**
  (Chin lift head tilt/jaw thrust)

Breathing →
- **Present and NORMAL** ☐ (between 10 & 30 breaths per minute)
- **Present NOT NORMAL** → ☐ → **EMERGENCY: Dial 999/112** (shallow/deep/rapid/slow/painful)
- **ABSENT** → CPR →

Circulation →
- No life-threatening bleeding ☐
- **LIFE-THREATENING BLEEDING:** → ☐ → **EMERGENCY: Dial 999/112**
  External bleeding
  Tummy tender/distended
  Broken pelvis/ thigh bone

CASUALTY EXAMINATION

Injuries Found

Description of Findings

Level of Response: **A C V P U**

Ask casualty or next of kin about **S A M P L E** (see overleaf)

First Aid Given	Time

Medication given/taken	Dose	Time

Pain score No Pain / Severe Pain **0 1 2 3 4 5 6 7 8 9 10**

MONITOR VITAL SIGNS	ACVPU = Alert Confused Voice Pain Unresponsive							
TIME								
A C V P U								
BREATHING RATE								
PULSE								
PAIN SCORE FROM 0-10								

ACTIVE FIRST AID   **www.activefirstaid.co.uk**

Index

Index